WEEDING
OUT THE
WANKERS

*Life and leadership lessons
from the workplace as seen
by a technology executive*

IBRAHIM GEDEON

To all the great people who made me who I am today and the wankers who made me realize I am truly blessed with wonderful friends and colleagues.

Table of Contents

Flashpoint — Why?

IT IS 11:46AM, MARCH 27, 2010 and I am sitting on a beach in Cancun smoking a cigar and asking myself "why am I writing this book?" The fact I had to think about it worried me a bit. After six serious revisions with feedback and support from friends, family, colleagues and my editor, I think a bit of laziness settled in. Also, I started questioning my personal motivation for doing this.

Let me tell you what I concluded. I believe success within any organization reinforces current behaviour, while failure forces change. Both success and failure, coupled together, provide us with the best of learning experiences. What I have observed, however, is that success gets talked about a whole lot more than failure. So I decided to capture some of the more difficult experiences I have had, and some of the key lessons I have learned from them, the most important of which is that we have to learn to recognize when things aren't working out. I have found that the identification of a "failed" situation is just as important as its mitigation. As with alcoholism, the first step to recovery is acceptance of inescapable truth.

One more thing: I am a big supporter of students, especially the ones doing so many amazing things in our business and engineering schools. If all that occurs as a result of my efforts is that a handful of recent graduates have some new things to think about as they take their first career steps, I'm a happy man.

I'll let you get back to the book as it was designed before I began re-evaluating the whole thing on this beach. Besides, it's almost time for lunch.

Preface

LIKE ALL MY NON-WORK PROJECTS, it took me forever to get this one done. If hobbies had deadlines, I would need 48 hours in the day. The old saying *tempus fugit* – time flies – grows increasingly resonant in my ears. And so I thought I should waste no more of it in finishing a project that a good friend tells me is "a highly non-conventional examination of a highly conventional subject."

Living in the corporate world for the past twenty years, I decided to put on paper some of the lessons I have learned as a subordinate, colleague and manager. I have read numerous management and leadership books, the themes of which are always about success stories and winners. What we rarely get is a book about the non-contributing personalities, misguided projects and misused tools we encounter, and how we can go about minimizing their impact on our lives. In my experience, it only takes one such employee – the proverbial bad apple – to spoil the bushel, turning the best high-performing team into an in-fighting and self-promoting group of individuals.

Before you read further, you should know that I am an engineer through and through, and I approach the world as an applied scientist – viewing problems and solutions as bookends. My professional turning point was in 1994 when I was a member of the scientific staff specializing in packet telephony at Nortel Networks, Canada's then technology superstar. I decided to abandon the "purity" of being a technical expert in my field to that of managing people. I joined the executive ranks in 1998, and since then, I have been a senior technology executive and have led numerous projects in concert with a number of large multinational organizations in the telecommunications technology field. Over the course of my consultations, reading, studies and practical experience, I believe that I've learned and experienced enough to justify offering others a bit of irreverent guidance through this book.

With deep respect to my friends and colleagues in the academic world, I hasten to emphasize that what appears in the following pages is not by any means a detailed scholarly examination of the various minefields one encounters in the realm of corporate leadership, but more like a light-hearted romp through them.

A word about the aforementioned management and leadership books, they all seem the same in the end. After the author concludes a series of detailed examples of a company's success and his or her own personal triumphs, the final pages then summarize the key points of wisdom, along with iron-clad assurances that the reader will inevitably experience similar success by simply following the recommendations. My hope is that this book will provide you with additional insights by examining not the best, but the realities in the corporate world. At the very least, I am confident that the capture of a few short hard lessons – conveniently learned by others – will provide you with a fresh view on how to recognize a few common pitfalls, be it in managing people or projects. In the end, I will let you be the judge if what I have captured is relevant and useful.

I should add at this point that if I really thought that the world needed another book about success stories and winners or magical success recipes, my task would have been much easier than the one I have committed to in the following pages. One easy task would simply have been to document the successful transformation of TELUS from a regionally based traditional telecom provider to a national provider and the strategic leader in Canadian telecommunications. While I contend that the TELUS story is one for the corporate history books, it is one that I will leave for others to tell. Besides, at the risk of being repetitive after only a few paragraphs, there is as much to be learned from failure as from success. And so, on we go.

The title is a humorous twist (I hope) on the term "wanker." The Oxford dictionary defines a wanker as "a contemptible or ineffectual person." Alternatively, and more colloquially, a wanker is British slang for someone that busies himself or herself with no results or gratification for others. During the earlier part of my career, whenever something or someone was deemed to be useless, we described it, or them, as wankers. I believe that was due to the high number of British engineers that I encountered in the early stages of my career in Canada. In choosing this title, I have drawn attention to the inevitability of being faced with self-indulged people and dubious projects at various points in our careers, highlighted the warning signs that tell us when something is wrong, and suggested proactive measures one can take to mitigate their ill effects.

In life, we will all make mistakes. I believe that anyone who has not made mistakes couldn't have taken any risks, and that no greatness occurs in the absence of risk taking and passion. The key is in how fast we recover from mistakes and re-align ourselves on the right path.

In terms of the organization of this book, it took me a long time to think about the best way to capture the material. I decided to organize it into three main sections: bad leadership, wasteful projects, and misused tools. I might as well tell you now, I like to throw numerous ideas around with anecdotes to capture certain points. The thoughts are all over the place, so I will not win any literary awards, but I am optimistic that the key messages have survived intact.

One more thing, I use military and sports analogies a lot, and I am told that these are sometimes politically incorrect. I say, why stop now? If they help to tell the story, use them.

And so what you have in your hands at this moment is a book about my management experiences, warts, hives, geek-speak, political incorrectness, and all. And in order to illustrate its points, it is purposely longer on catastrophe than on conquest. And as you can see, it is also rather condensed. Why write volumes when short sentences will do?

Please enjoy, ... ijg

"Brevity is the soul of wit."
— WILLIAM SHAKESPEARE, *Hamlet*, Act 2 Scene 2

CHAPTER I

Painting the Titanic
— Academic Leadership

I ONCE WROTE A MEMO titled "Painting the Titanic" effectively asking the question, when the ship is sinking, why would one continue with business as usual and occupy oneself with regular activities that do not help the bottom line? When times are suddenly precarious, a radical change in direction and leadership is sometimes a necessity. If you recall the movie Titanic, there is a scene that I will never forget, in which I believe the orchestra's conductor said "let's do what we do best," and the band played on while the Titanic was sinking. No doubt beautiful music, but I believe they could have done something else to support themselves and the passengers. Some out-of-the-box thinking, rather than more of the same might have been good. I am not sure, but perhaps a cello could have been used as a floatation device.

It is interesting that in corporate life (North America particularly) companies tend to set the path of their destruction in the name of recovery. If you look at companies like Nortel or General Motors, the executive teams did what they do best in bad times – more of the same. What I mean is that they went about optimizing their traditional business model rather than questioning its effectiveness. Sounds wrong? It is. It's critical to challenge the principle "do what you do best" when an organization is facing massive challenges from competition and its cost structure.

To illustrate, let's return for a moment to the decks of the stricken ship. Let's suppose that a team of painters was putting the finishing touches on the Titanic as she made her maiden voyage and that, immediately after hitting the iceberg, they opted to continue their painting in hopes that by doing what they do best, they might help to save the ship. Like the musicians, they were disciplined workers who remained focused on their areas of core competence in spite of a rather troubling occurrence. In hindsight, it seems fairly clear that neither the musicians nor the painters could have been able to save the Titanic irrespective of what actions they took. One thing that is certain though is that doing more of the same wouldn't have helped, irrespective of how efficiently they did it. New dynamics require a changed focus and realignment of resources to meet the new challenges.

The fact is that I have seen this tendency repeated more times than I care to remember. It seems the better the company is operated from a financial viewpoint, the more drawn out its demise. Cost cutting frequently appears to be an academic knee-jerk reaction, and it's typically spread across the entire organization rather than within strategically targeted areas. As the results have so far indicated, these companies are not likely to recover, and not from the lack of trying. I am by no means a learned business genius, just simply someone who has lived through numerous across-the-board cost cutting activities.

When a company engages in numerous rounds of cost cutting with no strategy, everything suffers equally and the biggest casualty is strategy itself and its pursuant long-term plans. These companies frequently experience short-lived recovery accompanied by a temporary lift in shareholder value, with "short-lived" and "temporary" being the key terms. Clients and shareholders are not that stupid and they tend to punish these organizations by losing confidence in their direction, products and long-term viability.

In my view, three things contribute to this slow and painful downward spiral. However, the reality is that no one wants to sink their ship, so I do not blame the hard working musicians, painters, food servers and deck hands, but rather the captain and officers.

I. IMPORTED EXECUTIVES WHO DO NOT REALLY UNDERSTAND THE BUSINESS

When times are good, appointing leaders from outside the industry with varied backgrounds can be great for both the organization and the leader. But as the tide turns, and it usually does, what is required is someone who keenly understands the business. Too often, a board of directors of a struggling company import a new leader from another business simply because he or she was successful there. These new leaders often do not understand their new industry, their new customers and their current and future needs, the technology and so on. Ultimately, their steep learning curve translates to a death spiral for an already struggling company. Alternatively, some organizations frequently and arbitrarily rotate leaders with varying backgrounds among various groups, thinking this can be positive for both the individual and the company, as it widens skill sets, builds management depth and brings new perspectives. This too can be risky. The practise of importing leaders from other fields and rearranging leadership chairs when corporate fortunes are on a downturn need to be vetted closely with clear business metrics to guide the way. For example, there are countless brilliant CFOS among corporations throughout the world, but precious few have turned the corner to become successful CEOS.

However, my personal view is that, regardless of the times, "academic leadership" or "imported leadership" – a term I use to describe leaders who have been put in place to gain new skills and perspective – is never desirable, and when someone is rotated to gain new experience, they should have a reasonable amount of time to do so, which is in most cases more than a year or two. I find too many of these rotations to be superficial moves in which the executives move on to the next rotation before their actions catch up with them. They are parachuted into a department, they make fundamental changes, rarely taking the time to understand things, and they move on before the longer term impacts of their actions are fully realized.

The most common occurrence is when an executive is parachuted in and their first action is to initiate a new process so they can understand what is happening, with no benefits to anyone but themselves. A wanker? Quite possibly. When someone shares a new strategy and puts in place an execution plan, business metrics such as cost and overall effort and benefits should be pointed out. In addition, senior leaders of large organizations are rarely able to invoke any meaningful change in less than two years.

All too often they rely upon academic logic and philosophies; an excellent starting point, but the applicability to the specific corporation is sometimes lacking. For example, I am weary of statements such as "we will exit businesses in which we have less than 20 per cent market share, or businesses in which we are not in the top three." You would think that given the average CEO's salary of a few million dollars a year, they would have more depth and insight in selecting their business criteria.

My own belief is that success can be achieved in a crowded market in which companies have less than 20 per cent market share, or in which they are not in the top three. The Apple iPhone, which clearly defined a new space in mobile devices, had less than two per cent of market share in 2009, yet they were more profitable than Nokia, the largest device manufacturer in the world.

The car rental and restaurant industries are good examples of the survival of numerous players. The market is enormous and therefore a ten per cent stake can be hugely profitable. We are seeing some consolidation in these industries, but the leaders know their clients and seem to be able to handle changing economic times. I could be proven wrong, but they seem to have managed to realign in step with economic cyclicality.

In any case, what happens when leaders with great track records are brought in to transform a company, the question invariably becomes: transform it to what? Once that question is answered, the most important requirement is a strategy to guide the transformation. Business transformation and the realignment of process, structure and culture are all great, however one needs a solid and understandable business strategy, accompanied by a portfolio of sellable products and services to successfully navigate through the necessary change management procedures and invoke new and improved processes.

Mike Zafarofski (last CEO of Nortel Networks – a former Fortune 500 company) publicly pondered if what was ailing his company was his fault. My belief is that he was chiefly responsible, but I also believe that the Board of Directors was at fault too. I am sure this view might surprise many, as we rarely hold directors accountable. History proved that he was simply the last in a series of wrong CEOs for the job. The Board should have questioned their selection criteria and looked for someone who could save the company. Instead, they put their faith in a guy who was brilliant as a leader of a mobile devices business unit (Zaforoski was a superstar senior executive at Motorola and led the team that developed the Razor phone), but he was not knowledgeable about the telecommunications infrastructure business. The fundamental question here is would a guy who builds cars be the best guy to build roads? It seems in the highest offices, Boards naively believe that a good CEO of a plumbing company can save a troubled car manufacturer or a telecommunications equipment manufacturer.

The point is simply that, in hard times, you need someone with a clear understanding of the space in which the organization operates. I do not subscribe to the belief that a good sales person can sell anything. They may have the mechanics of the sales process down to a tee, but the knowledge of how a product is applied and the culture surrounding how one would buy it is rarely the same between various industrial segments.

So, when leaders are brought in that do not know the industry and its culture, they tend to apply what they know best: objectively observing what is going wrong and then coming in, often as consultants, with clear ideas on how to fundamentally re-align the business model and products, and implementing tough enterprise-wide changes.

The problem is that there is a huge demarcation between knowing what should work, and knowing how to operationalize it. When highly generalized recommendations are not applied to the specifics and actual situation of the organization, they tend to fail. The usual mode of operations is that the surviving leadership team tends to clam up and make the newcomers' lives difficult. In response, these imported leaders either leave or they "go native," which in today's corporate vernacular means that they simply conform to the status quo and join the others in watching the ship sink further.

In an international corporation, knowing the business and the specific space in which the organization operates includes understanding cultural variances between various markets. Let's face it; there are very few Carlos Ghosns in the world so simply replicating his model without taking into account his personal contribution is a formula for disaster.

Just in case you are not familiar with Carlos Ghosn, he is the President and CEO of Renault-Nissan. He is an Argentinean of Lebanese origin working for a French company. There is a book, *The Medici Effect,* by Frans Johansson, which explains how people who bridge numerous cultural experiences are great innovators. Carlos Ghosn is, in my view, a superb case in point. Before he became CEO, he was given the task of streamlining Nissan and turning it into a profitable enterprise.

Numerous books were written on the success of Carlos Ghosn. His success boiled down to knowing the business and accommodating the differences in culture both on the production line and among the end-users. At the end of the day, car manufacturing in Japan differs from car manufacturing in France. Numerous similarities exist on the actual automotive platform, but the approach is completely different, as are the work habits and norms of the workers who build the cars and the customers who buy them.

Knowing how and where to cut costs is also a fundamental prerequisite to informed leadership. Proper cost cutting means abandoning specific things rather than spreading targets across all parts of the organization, which often indicates a blatant lack of understanding as to what will be the growth and innovation engines. Most leadership-challenged organizations tend to look at exiting businesses only after numerous rounds of painful and ineffective cost cutting.

In the early 2000s, John Chambers, the CEO of Cisco Systems, went about the task of downsizing, and his message to the troops was that he would cut once, swiftly and surgically. As a corporation, Cisco went through only one round of formal layoffs, although they continuously focus on exiting low performers. There is no doubt that the strategy of cutting once worked for them and saved the employees and clients from the constant fear of downsizing, and increased the potential for the company's longevity.

2. INERT LEADERSHIP

These are those leaders one might encounter whose decisions and actions are visible, but their underlying rational is unclear or non-existent. In some cases, they have become mere messengers, taking directives from their bosses, subordinates or consultants, and then simply passing them on down to their direct reports, without adding any value in the form of guidance on how to achieve new objectives, or without challenging their wisdom. In other words, the value they add as leaders amounts to nothing. My advice if you are faced with such a leader, and you feel you are not progressing, is to look for opportunities elsewhere.

Bad times require both regrouping operationally and making proper investments, which means investments in what will change the fortunes of a company. Improving efficiency and cost cutting are but one tool. They must be coupled with investment in the future, or else slow death is the typical misfortune.

A good example from the telecommunication industry of a proper reaction to bad times is Ericsson during the Dot Com collapse. Rather than cutting their research and development funding, they doubled it, focusing on wireless networks and systems. Today they are the global leader. I hate beating a dead horse, but Nortel's continuous kneejerk belt tightening was the beginning of the end.

I have been around enough of these types of leaders to conclude that the rationale for their decisions and actions are rooted in the sheer desire to save their own skin or ensure they are blameless. They ignore obvious signs of trouble within the organization. Their efforts, if you can call them that, are typically of no consequence. And the result is managerial inertia, with either nothing being accomplished in spite of executive actions, or nothing being accomplished because nothing is even being seriously attempted among executives who are essentially trying to find a hiding place to wait out the storm. It is when a few iterations of cost cutting imperatives arise that they are often flushed out and seen for what they truly are.

Usually after a few rounds of cost cutting, a number of executive team members are let go and a number of others leave of their own volition. No doubt some low performers are let go, but often good leaders that want fundamental change and realignment of the organization are also let go or they leave in frustration. The reasons are numerous, but the most popular official explanation is they are not seen as a team players.

After a couple of years of cost cutting without a clear strategy, I have observed that two prominent behaviours tend to emerge among the remaining executive ranks. The first behaviour is a strong instinct for survival. The remaining executives do not lack intelligence, but are focused on job preservation and doing what they do best, which is professional management and not leadership. This results in rallying around tactics and not strategy, as the company focuses on things like new procedures and behaviour retraining, and not on essentials such as new products, services or customers.

The second behaviour is appearing blissfully ignorant and toeing the corporate line. They may know things are in a downward spiral, but manage to convince themselves otherwise and embrace cosmetic change, which provides false hope and not fundamental change. In so doing, they are choosing to be lords of a crumbling empire. Strange, but some people would rather be the King of Iceland than US Secretary of State. Egos and titles are the common pitfalls of the great. I guess this all started with Julius Caesar when he defeated the Gauls. When one of his generals made fun of the defeated King of the Gauls, saying he was in the corner cowering like a dog, Julius Caesar declared: "better the King of Gaul than the second man in Rome." That must have been one of the first title-before-power statements documented in history.

I mentioned earlier that I tend to use a lot of sport and military analogies, but as you can see, I am also somewhat of a historian at heart. In fact, I wanted to become a historian after high school. Thankfully my uncle (Jiryis Shammas) sat me down and told me to get a degree that would provide me with a steady and lucrative income and take history on as a hobby. Well you know what I became, and for that I am ever grateful to him. I do not want to propose, however, that people should focus strictly on their core competence and not expand their horizons in other fields. There is no doubt that expansive knowledge is both personally satisfying and a great asset, but it's best to first know the stuff that earns you a living, and then diversify. But I digress.

When the overall leadership team becomes inert, they simply execute without being impeded by any kind of thoughtful analysis of potential outcomes. I know inert leadership is a harsh term, but the description fits here. They stop mapping out realistic scenarios for the corporation and actually act like the ship is sunk and they are making the best of it while it lasts. The similarities between good military leaders and good business leaders are remarkable. In my opinion, Britain's General Montgomery – "Monty" to his legions of admirers – was a model leader because he always made it a priority to map out worst-case scenarios and put plans in place that could be undertaken if in fact the worst case unfolded in whatever theatre of war he happened to be commanding troops.

During World War II, Montgomery was the Allied Forces commander in Africa. When faced with the impending attack on the British forces in Egypt, he mapped out the worst case scenario. He assumed that the Germans would take Egypt and Palestine and therefore planned a retreat for the Golan Heights in Syria. I doubt that wishfully thinking that the Germans would stumble would have been the right strategy, or "let's do what we do best" without any planning would have worked. Thankfully, the Germans never entered Cairo and the rest is history. It was not that he was pessimistic, but a realist planning for all outcomes. So in corporate life, doing half measures hoping things will improve seems to be leadership wishing for luck. Does anyone want to be part of such an organization?

In many cases, it is interesting to note that with the firing or abandonment of the executive ranks in an organization, few members remain who toiled and championed to make the organization great. I've never thought that to be particularly surprising, since the best people tend to have the greatest number of options elsewhere.

I would venture that none of the folks who risked their careers at Nortel to build the world's first digital switch or the world's first 10-Gigabit Optical switch are still there, and no they are not 100 years old. I remain a fan of John Roth, the Nortel CEO who was blamed for so many things. Hindsight being 20–20, the man was perhaps a lousy CEO, and once the 2000 bust came around Nortel suffered more than most. I contend though that he knew what Nortel was all about and would have seen the company through, rather than being the first in a revolving door of CEOs that Nortel employed. I know he had his faults, but he was instrumental in making Nortel a global player and not just a Canadian regional equipment manufacturer. His track record as a CEO remains dismal, but the man clearly knows the space, the clients and the corporate culture. I am sure lots of people were involved in these successes, but clearly the few leaders that had the vision and the courage to bet their careers on these two projects (digital switching and optical transport) are long gone from Nortel. I have no doubt that the Nortel executive alumni would disagree, as they are a good and intelligent group of people, but they appeared to manage by continuing to do what they did best and by staying with old strategies and incremental technology evolution rather than being guided by where the new technology was going and what the customers actually needed.

3. WAITING FOR DIVINE INTERVENTION

Perhaps this section should be called, "hopeful planning." Actually I was a bit lost on how to describe those leaders that fall into this category. They are the folks that take the best case scenario as the one that is highly probable. They are typically in two camps, one that cannot predict the competition and the market, and one that allies itself with luck. They differ from the inert variety in that they truly have mapped out a strategy for success and are willing to be held more accountable for their actions. Their downfall, however, is the inability to be realistic about what to expect.

The ones that cannot predict the competition are similar to the world's leaders in World War II. They assumed after every Nazi conquest, Hitler would stop. First came the annexation of Austria, after which the leaders of other countries convinced themselves it was a local matter. Then came the annexation of Czechoslovakia, and again they convinced themselves it was another local matter. I would like to add that, had Poland not had a joint defence agreement with France, then the invasion of Poland would have been considered an internal German matter too. One would think that the invasion of France would have clearly signalled that Hitler had predatory ambitions.

US President Roosevelt clearly saw the Nazi threat from the onset. Even though the attack on Pearl Harbour formalized the entry of the US into World War II, the Americans were in it way before as advisors and weapons suppliers. I am not being dramatic here, for the truth is that in corporate life, we are at war with our competition. Other than government services, there remain few monopoly industries. To bring this point back to its origin, waiting for the Germans to indicate they were satisfied with their wins or for their soldiers to be hit with the plague seems a touch optimistic as a strategy for the Allies.

The other camp in this section is that of the ever optimistic leaders who ally themselves with luck. If you have ever been part of a complex project, you have experienced the complexity and dependencies between the tasks, and at some stage in the planning, you also examined the spectrum of potential outcomes ranging from best case to worst case scenarios. From my experience with large and complex projects, the people involved should consider themselves lucky if the average case scenario of the combined tasks occurs. Yet the leaders in this category seem to be hopelessly optimistic and assume the best scenario for each task is the most likely reality. Not only do they convince themselves, but they also convince others that this is the normal expectation. And as we know, this rarely happens, so they are disappointed that their unrealistic expectations were not met and dish out punishment according to their warped perceptions.

Maybe I should call these leaders "the gamblers." Gambling with an organization's wealth, intellectual property and employees must be the ultimate thrill for an addicted gambler. Why bankrupt yourself and your family when you can do that to thousands of people?

An example in this category is the CEO of British Petroleum, Tony Hayward, who was clearly hoping that the oil spill in the Gulf of Mexico would simply blow over. Too little; too late, and now he has resigned with an $18 million exit package. Another would be Bernie Madhoff and the schemes he was running, using new money to salvage the old and ending up losing $70 billion worth of investments.

BOOKENDS AND WHAT IFS

Neville Chamberlain

Optimism is great, and hope is a fantastic driver, but reality must never be abandoned for the sake of either. I believe when most people embark on these magical leadership formulas they rarely capture a scenario for when the "formula" does not work. Forgive me for resorting to the same military analogy, but the position of Great Britain in World War II is a good example. Let me explain. Neville Chamberlain was prime minister of Britain when World War II broke out, although

Chamberlain declared world peace in 1938 after meeting with Hitler. Was it the wine, the good company, or was the guy simply delusional to have failed to recognize the grim reality of what was unfolding in Europe? I think we all know what happened in 1939 with the invasion of Poland. But the people of England, effectively duped by their leader, treated the earlier annexation of Austria and the invasion of Czechoslovakia as sad events, but ultimately internal German matters. The reality of the matter was that Britain and the rest of the world soon came to realize they were fighting for their existence, and that drastic matters required drastic measures. It had become impossible to believe that Germany's interest was solely Europe, and that Britain was safe.

"How horrible, fantastic, incredible it is that we should be digging trenches and trying on gas-masks here because of a quarrel in a far-away country between people of whom we know nothing!"
— NEVILLE CHAMBERLAIN

There can be no doubt that in announcing "Peace for our time" to the people of England, Neville Chamberlain was terribly naïve. It was, I think, simply a case of wishful thinking, rather than a realistic estimation of how great the danger was for his fellow citizens and the rest of the world.

This naiveté is analogous to corporate CEOS who live quarter to quarter with no long term thought, and remain forever stuck hoping the world around them will make things right, rather than participating in their companies and mapping their future.

Similar to Chamberlain, executives are often similarly reluctant to position the true and realistic bookend – the cold hard truth. True, nobody likes doom and gloom scenarios, but the prospects of breaking up a company or being taken over is a realistic outcome that has to be considered. Yes, I am a Nortel Networks alumnus and it pains me that a Canadian and Global telecommunications giant has been split up and sold in pieces. In hind sight, doing this in 2005 would have been better for shareholders, employees and customers. The alternative is "death by duck bites," a suitable saying that captures pathetic companies that "do more of the same," rather than confront realities.

The car industry in North America also lends a few good examples. General Motors' Saturn initiative was designed to compete against the Japanese car onslaught on the North American market. GM invested in Japan to create Saturn, sadly six or more years in the making, and they only succeeded in creating a car that competed with the North American car manufacturers. The big hope and optimism was that all was well, and that Saturn would save the day, but as we know it was a dismal failure. Not only do these executives do more of the same, they do it more efficiently. Looking at the big picture, we can see that these companies tend to simply dig themselves deeper into trouble. I am sure many books will be written by academics and executives on the North American car industry, which waited too long to address the labour and pension situations, never mind sagging quality. After 20 years in decline, they finally decided to tackle these issues, but as history may yet tell us, it will have been too late. They failed to believe the good times might never come back. They simply assumed that the economy was growing and they didn't have to address their cost of manufacturing and quality issues. However, I must give full credit to Ford Motor Company, which seems to be more intent than the other Big Two North American car manufacturers in reinventing itself.

I find that in life the choices we make lead us down certain paths and we can rarely recreate the good old days. I believe there is an old Chinese proverb about how life is like going through a series of one-way doors. Even if we succeed in taking ourselves back, the reality is that things have moved on and evolved.

One of the reasons leaders do not position the true and realistic bookend could be attributed to three things:

1 They simply do not know what the worst outcome may be, General Bill Owen as CEO of Nortel was a good example

2 They are worried about internal and external perceptions, Frank Dunn is a good example here as the whole world saw Nortel's fortunes declining and he kept indicating times were improving; and I recall when they paid out bonuses during his reign.

3 They simply believe whatever it is that they want to believe, a highly common human flaw, more on Neville Chamberlain.

If you go around asking employees at struggling corporations, I doubt they will buy that the world is beautiful when it clearly isn't. Corporations need realistic leaders in bad times, as people are inclined to rally around honesty and commonality of destinies in such times. Chamberlain lost the confidence of the British people because he was unrealistic about Nazi Germany. He kept waiting to see that the light at the end of the tunnel was actually Nazi expansion. No doubt the British Empire at that time was facing many challenges in India and Palestine and he wanted to avoid additional conflict; this goes to the point of not being able to prioritize what conflict to tackle first. My point here is simply this: if the leader appears to be dreaming, ask yourself, what if? When much is at stake, look at the potential of things going wrong and how you would recover. A leader should be able to assess what are the most important aspects of the challenges facing the corporation. To do so requires intimacy with all of the organization's resources, needs and capabilities.

YOSHI MINEGISHI

I think we have talked enough about bad leadership, so I thought I would capture a rare example of leadership accountability and loyalty.

The year was 1996, and I was the manager of the systems engineering team for Nortel's data networks division. My role was global at that time and I had the opportunity to support Nortel's thrusts in many markets and Japan was one of them. I was sitting in my office when I received a letter from Minegishi san (Yoshi Minegishi – then President of Nortel Japan). The letter simply stated that he, as the head of Nortel Japan, had failed to meet the stated objectives of the organization over two years, and with that in mind, he tendered his resignation to the CEO of Nortel. His letter went on to thank all the people who supported him and wished them well in their careers, but he and he alone took the sole blame for the failure of meeting the objectives in Japan.

By North American standards, Nortel Japan was profitable and doing well, so it seemed peculiar that he would resign. It is typically more common in such situations to either dress the pig (paint a rosier picture than the one that was apparent) or finds something extraordinary to blame for the failure. Many would say Menegishi san ran away from the challenges, but I believe that he gave himself a year, extended for another and when he failed to achieve his objectives, he voluntarily moved aside.

I am fortunate to have known and worked with Menegishi san. More importantly, I am fortunate to have witnessed the ultimate in leadership and accountability.

SUMMARY

Life is about choices, so choose wisely about what kind of a leader you want to follow, or what kind of an organization you want to serve. The right leadership makes the difference in both good times and in bad. In your work life, you will have many leaders. No matter where you are in the organization, you should know what kind of leaders they are. I also believe that it is important to know what you want to get out of an organization and your leadership team. Knowing who controls your destiny is important.

It is not about the painters or musicians, but about leaders who cannot appreciate and gauge what their resources are capable of under perilous times. Legacy and academic leaders seem incapable of innovative thinking and bless people under their command with more of the same.

Leadership is about personal accountability and loyalty to the organization's shareholders and its people, not about having the privilege to negotiate a lucrative exit package when things go badly. Whether the gesture is idle or not, leaders who do not take a bonus or draw a salary during bad times are showing empathy with the organization, employees and clients. These gestures are not lost. Sadly though, we see more and more leaders that fight for an exit package in a sinking ship rather than sharing the fate of the people they led. CEOs, like the rest of us have to think of themselves, but the price of leadership includes additional responsibility such as the destiny of those one leads.

The ability to prioritize, mobilize, build effective teams and be accountable is what makes a great leader.

So when the leadership team in bad times introduces a new process that does not improve the company's competitive advantage in terms of products and services, they are wankers.

And when the leadership team presents a simple formula for recovery and success in a complex situation, they too are wankers. There are no easy solutions for complex problems.

When the leadership team is optimistic without having a realistic view and mitigation plans, they must be considered to be wankers.

When the leadership team is getting massive bonuses while your pay is being cut, chances are you are working for wankers.

Without a hint of doubt, when the leaders blame everyone but themselves for failures, they are textbook wankers.

When your leaders blame their leaders for unsound strategy and poor execution, you are truly beholden to wankers of the lowest order.

And if you happen to work in such an organization, I recommend you get out when you can, and the sooner the better, lest you too become a wanker.

"Bad news isn't wine. It doesn't improve with age."
— COLIN POWELL

CHAPTER 2

Michael Jordan strikes out
—Average Leadership

**MICHAEL JORDAN MINOR LEAGUE
BASEBALL STATISTICS**

Birmingham Barons AA (Chicago White Sox)
POSITION: Outfield. **BATTED:** Right.
THREW: Right. **HOW OBTAINED:** Signed as a
free agent by the White Sox on Feb. 7, 1994.
RETIRED FROM BASEBALL: Mar. 10, 1995.
JERSEY NUMBER: 45.

Michael Jordan

YEAR	AVG	GM	AB	R	H	TB	2B	3B	HR	RBI	BB	SO	SB	E
1994	.202	127	436	46	88	116	17	1	3	51	51	114	30	11

**ONE OF THE GREATEST BASKETBALL PLAYERS EVER KNOWN.
AS A BASEBALL PLAYER, NOT SO TERRIBLY GOOD.**

My struggle with being "well rounded" started when I had failing
grades in Arabic Literature. I used to struggle for a passing grade in
Arabic, which always lowered my overall grade-point average. I usually

aced my math, physics and chemistry courses, but failed most of my Arabic tests. Even though Arabic was my first language, I had never properly learned it, as I was enrolled in English and American schools most of my life. I remember the first time I passed a mid-term in Arabic Literature. The year was 1979, and I was in fourth intermediate – grade 10 equivalent in North America – and our teacher at that time, Mr. Hwallah, asked the class to give me a standing ovation. Later, I moved into the scientific track and Arabic literature was marginalized and completely phased out for Grade 13 (Baccalaureate Part II – I did my high school in Lebanon which adopted the French system).

Like a lot of people, I had great strengths, and great weaknesses. Schools and universities realized long ago that people are unique and certain elements should cater to their uniqueness. Academic programs all have core infrastructural elements, but they fundamentally cater to the individuals' strengths, particularly as one enters university and starts specializing in a certain field. The grade-point average remains ever so important, however, the mix of what makes up that average is fully customizable, and the higher the level of education, the more personalized it has become.

In our work life, we have taken on the notion of the grade-point average – normalized performance metrics – and applied it to our skill sets and experiences. When I joined the workforce, the human resource folks always encouraged employees to become "well rounded." Well rounded was a generic term to describe having a number of proven experiences, and the reason people cared about being well rounded was simply for recognition, a salary increase, or greater job security.

Remember how I started this chapter with my Arabic literature experience? Well, needing a passing grade for the final exam, I always spent more than 50 per cent of my time on Arabic literature so I could pass. A failing grade meant summer school and another series of exams. So while everyone was enjoying the beach, I was investing additional time on something I will never be good at or needed to be good at.

So, was it a good investment or a waste of time? I would like to be clear here; I am a firm believer that knowledge in general is an investment in oneself, but I also believe that you must first focus on what will make you successful and to distinguish that from other forms of knowledge that may be comparatively inconsequential within the greater context of life.

I remember when I did my bachelor's degree in Engineering at the American University of Beirut; we had to take an elective course in non-technical domains every trimester. We all used to wonder why the hell we would be forced to take a course every semester in Humanities and Arts when we were studying to become engineers. Actually, it turned out to be a good thing. That single course forced our interaction with other students in different fields to ensure we were well rounded and could relate to other areas. Yes, that elective course in Arts and Humanities did count towards our overall performance, but it was one course of six, a far cry from Arabic at school which included literature along with history and geography that were also in Arabic.

When I immigrated to Canada, I discovered that engineering students were allowed to take their electives in any domain including scientific areas. Having had an alternate experience, I think that was a loss for those students, one that helped to produce what I refer to – with no disrespect – as "the Great North American Geek effect." We on the other hand had to take a "compulsory elective" – an oxymoron of the highest order – of a series of courses called "civilization sequence," which basically translated to the study of human civilization through various literature artefacts in history. Studying the evolution of civilization as we know it, who knew that the epic of Gilgamesh written a few thousand years ago was the trigger? Did this help make me a better engineer? Probably not, but a more rounded person for sure, and hopefully a somewhat better dinner conversationalist. Training of the mind, logic, sense, confidence, and power of comparison are an asset for all aspects of life, but they should be complimented with the training of core skills and their utilization.

VERY AVERAGE PEOPLE ARE SUPERBLY WELL ROUNDED

It is true, average people tend to be well rounded. What the sports world and academia recognized a long time ago is just catching up with industry. You would never have Pelé the great Brazilian football striker play goalie, nor would you have Roger Federer play football (even though Roger stated he loved it as a child). I am sure they both could, but would be lousy.

While being well rounded was once a key thrust in people development at large organization, it has been more recently noticed that this should not happen at the expense of individuals losing their competitive strengths and an understanding of how those can be applied to an organization. As a result, I have seen some new thrusts in management. For example, the Gallup organization has some new publications and testing around finding an individual's strengths, and playing those up rather making their weaknesses go away. The book *Strength Finder* by Tom Rath, with all the related flavours, is good. I believe Gallup has gone Strength Finder crazy though, with screening for kids and trying to start a new paradigm with Strength Finder based leadership. I think the book and directions are great, and if a new industry and new management and leadership styles emerge, good for them. However, we have not arrived at the level of maturity in the workplace to accept failure in certain tasks and experiences. Humans are ever the optimists. Let me explain.

The impact of grooming a junior person is typically well contained. The damage they will inflict if their results are suboptimal is minimal. Usually when someone starts, they are handed well defined problems and have numerous checks and balances. This is the time for them to make mistakes and learn. The travesty is when an accomplished executive is being groomed for greater things and the corporation undertakes the task of "rounding" them. I find that rarely works. I am pretty sure they will be accomplished, well-spoken and able to "run things," but is that what we want? Where are the business leadership and the quest to increase market share and earnings? How do the reasons for an organization's very existence suddenly become so marginalized? Why would one's core competencies and chosen areas of expertise suddenly become anchors rather than rallying skills when they are rotated around at a very senior level in the corporation?

Typically, you will have one of four outcomes when people are rotated at a senior level – the dreaded "well-rounding" exercise that is still undertaken by many large corporations.

1 **Success** is the rarest of outcomes, especially if these individuals are superstars. This is an indication of their ability to work with the teams they inherited and applying their core strengths to whatever role they have. Carlos Ghosn is a great example here, and another is Jules Meunier, the previous head of Wireless Products and Services at Nortel Networks.

2 **The perception of success** is one of the more common outcomes. I do not have statistical evidence of this; I recommend you look at the experiences around you. Usually these individuals are folks who believe they are superstars and have been fast-tracked early in life; be it because they were competent or simply eloquent is irrelevant. In general, these individuals are famous for outpacing the results of their work. They tend to change and modify roles and processes and change jobs before their track record catches up with them. I have to say these are individuals with high IQs who know how to work the system. They also tend to overhaul their executive team when they take over and redesign

everything, making it difficult to track their performance from previous metrics – smart! People need to pay their dues so they can properly learn from their experiences.

3 **Failure** is another rare case, as failure is something that is rarely acknowledged, but rather typically attributed to the organization as a whole. And, let's not forget, we are again starting with intelligent people who can manipulate or have been manipulating corporate intelligence for a long time. Frank Dunn, the previous CEO of Nortel and a very nice man, fits the bill here. He was by all standards a brilliant innovator in the financial modelling arena, but as the record attests, not a terribly good CEO.

4 **Average at best** is the most common outcome. These senior leaders have had enough management experience to ensure that they keep the organization afloat, though not necessarily moving it forward. These individuals move from superstars, to superstars who are undertakers at best. Another Nortel example comes to mind here, General Bill Owen. He was honest, intelligent, hardworking, but had no clue about the telecom business, and much less about working with customers. Perhaps the military training and his level of rank was to blame, as his only client was the joint chief of staff and the military organization – not ideal leadership training for a multi-national equipment provider.

I maintain that having Wayne Gretzky play goalie before he assumed the role of captain of the Edmonton Oilers back in the 1980's was not something any coach would have considered. So why do corporations so misunderstand what sports teams have known forever? I have a lot of respect for Michael Jordan. He had the guts to try baseball, but I admire him more for also having the guts to admit defeat as a baseball player. You will note that his rotation into another sport was in a minor league baseball team. How many times have we seen a senior executive taking a management rotation in a demoted role in another area? Very rare. Still, there is no doubt Michael Jordan was a great basketball player and superb athlete, but he proved to be a pretty lousy baseball player. Check out his statistics at the beginning of this chapter.

ROTATION DONE RIGHT IS THE BEST FORM OF PROMOTION

I believe that after reading this chapter, you will think I am dead against rotation. Actually I think rotation is a fantastic commitment by the organization towards individuals earmarked as super stars. It is the right move to widen these individuals' understanding of all aspects of the business. In so doing, the corporation is building its senior executive farm team, which is important, but the key is to manage rotations properly.

Here are some basic questions that must be asked about rotations.

1   Is this a temporary assignment to fill a gap or a valid role that requires new talent and leadership?

2   Does the person being rotated want the role? Sometimes people do what is expected of them rather than what they want. Personal satisfaction is a valuable thing.

3   Does the rotation have an element of the individual's strengths? As a senior executive reading spread sheets and being well spoken are necessary skills, but not sufficient for running a business unit. What are the other elements that a person brings to the role is the question.

4   The more senior the person involved in the rotation, the longer the rotation time should be. At a senior level, one would expect

the leader to impact strategy and not just "manage" people and operations on a day to day basis. To actually learn and make substantive contributions in a large organization, one would need two to three years for the effects to be realized. When one refines the strategy and sets things in place, including process, the success and failure cannot be based on academic plans, but rather on business metrics and real-life feedback, for which one would typically allow two to three years.

5   What is the rotation program feedback mechanism? Does anyone get demoted or do they get moved out or moved around? If these individuals are super stars, it seems a travesty to render them inert because the rotation failed. As leaders are changed the expectations should be reset, and the opportunity for new blood in certain roles should be accompanied by business metrics.

I would like to share a few examples that I personally witnessed. Steve Schilling was the senior executive at Nortel responsible for North American Sales. I can personally say that he was one of the most talented leaders to ever run Sales. Steve started his career as a sales engineer, and later moved into Sales in the telephony CPE organization at Nortel (basically selling key systems to businesses). In the mid 1990's, a number of people at Nortel, including myself, felt he could be the next CEO. At Nortel, almost every CEO had a stint as a product head, so the logical next step was to give Steve a product organization. Steve was given the Access division, and at that time Nortel was the global pioneer in broadband connectivity over copper (the pre-cursor to DSL with their product called the 1 Meg Modem). Two years into his role, and almost a billion dollars in R&D later, Nortel not only lost its leadership position, but was also overtaken by its competitors, such as Alcatel, which had entered the DSL business. To Steve's credit, he went back and accepted a sales role, but the damage to Nortel was irreversible and they abandoned the broadband wire-line access business.

Done right, rotation is great, but in my experience, done right is the exception rather than the norm.

SUMMARY

Play to your strengths. Recognize and hone your core skills. Beware of initiatives designed to round a person's skill set at the expense of their core competence. Also, be aware that one person does not make a team. Singles tennis is not a team sport, and rarely are corporate endeavours a one-person effort. Someone will always have to lead, but you need all the skill-sets on a team to be successful and deliver.

Embrace change of scope in your job, but always know what you are contributing and what your value is. As you move from role to role, you bring a wealth of experience. It is up to you if you will use that experience as a launching pad in the new role, or as a boat anchor.

Don't let your ego get out of control. I myself have succumbed to the evils of an incurable ego. In 1998 I had the Global Engineering team for Nortel's data products. Our team at that time had an excellent relationship from the core product group with our key customers. When we were re-aligning to provide more product focus to our regional offices and it was proposed that the regional sales support teams should report to me, I did not hesitate one second to accept the assignment. I have to admit, the acceptance was a result of my ego and I was fortunate enough to have a great global team that educated me and supported me to turn my technical knowledge and the key customer relationships into a winning combination. I am hesitant to say that my rotation was successful, however, the results were apparently good, and I personally learned the difference between back office support as a roaming global expert and being in the thick of things when one's livelihood depends on customer support and sales.

So if you are asked to do something to which you will clearly not contribute value, you are working for a wanker or you have become one yourself.

If someone is in a new role for more than a year with no measurable contribution, this is a warning sign that they may well be a wanker.

If your leader's contribution is a new process that does not help things, he or she is a wanker.

And if you are asked to play a different role, be truthful to yourself, or risk becoming a wanker.

"Hide not your talents. They for use were made.
What's a sundial in the shade?"
— BENJAMIN FRANKLIN

CHAPTER 3:

Empathy and Sympathy
— know the difference!

I WAS ACTUALLY NOT SURE where I would address this subject, whether it will be a stand-alone chapter or part of chapter one on leadership skills. Empathy and sympathy are human traits that I believe are needed at all levels, however, for leaders, empathy is the more valuable skill. I believe it is people's inability to understand the difference between these two traits and the misuse of one over the other that moved me to dedicate a chapter on this topic. It really is about communication with the right emotion at the appropriate time.

In order to fully understand the subtle difference, let's begin by asking ourselves a question: how many times have we attended a presentation or seminar, supposedly geared to us, only to be completely bored out of our skulls and not get the message the presenter is trying to convey? Every presenter's intention is to communicate, yet many fail to do so effectively. The communication game gets even trickier for anyone working in an international business environment. As the world is shrinking, and English increasingly becomes the language of business and technology, the varying cultures, customs and interpretations present new communication challenges.

It never ceases to amaze me how humans formulate their logic and communication tactics. English is my first learned language, yet I speak Arabic and French. I tend to formulate the phrase in English, and intuitively translate it to the intended target language. I tell you, there is a difference. For example, if you formulate your sentences in Arabic and translate literally to another language – say English – the result may seem bizarre, even though it is perfectly fine in Arabic. On a humorous note, the slang word for smoking in Arabic is "drink," so one formulating the sentence in Arabic and translating to English can easily "drink a cigarette."

Another example of cultural disconnect occurred to me while shopping in France. We North Americans are used to going into a store and asking for what we want, and in fact, anything else is considered a sign of not knowing what we want. In France, the approach and determinism so valued in North America may be construed as rude and obnoxious. Actually, in France the sales people in a shop are meant to help you to solve a problem, and they define their jobs as being able to come up with solutions. Even if you know what you want, then you should ask for their help in solving your problem within the required parameters. If you do so, you will be surprised with how helpful they are and how easily you get what you want. What would work in a shop demonstrating cultural differences also works in a restaurant; for example, if you are in a hurry and go to a French restaurant and tell them, as we North Americans often do, that you are in a hurry and need to be served quickly, you will inevitably piss them off. On the other hand, if you tell the waiter you have a pressing engagement in an hour and would appreciate his help in getting a meal and making your engagement, you will get the quick service and a suggestion for dishes that do not take too much time. *Voilà la différence!*

Cultural issues aside, the truth is that people tend to capture and share information in a format that makes sense to them. This is often a mistake, because the first key of effective communication is understanding how the audience thinks and absorbs knowledge. I have been in numerous meetings where the audience is just not tuned in, often because it is so easy for presenters to incorrectly interpret their body language. The larger the audience, the more difficult it gets. This is the reason that I believe keynote speeches should not last more than 30 minutes, and that the key messages must apply directly to the audience (not withstanding Pierre Trudeau's or Fidel Castro's hours-long addresses to parliament or the people). If one looks at successful keynote speakers, they tend to be generic with a limited number of key themes, yet prolific with specific relevant anecdotes to help the audience relate to the key themes.

"I showed them" is a phrase I will never forget. During my graduate studies at Carleton University, one of my colleagues presented his research to the engineering faculty and students. My feedback was honest and I stated that it was far too complex and that I would bet most of the attendees had no clue what he was talking about. He told me, "I showed them how much I know about the topic." He honestly saw no issue in the fact he communicated nothing to his audience; actually he was pleased with himself. If your objective in a presentation is to demonstrate how much more you know about a topic than your audience, I believe there are better vehicles than a presentation. Communication is about communicating, and empathy with the audience is critical. When dealing and communicating with people, language and cultural translation are critical for success.

SYMPATHY

My good friend Anne Raymond asked me why this section is in here, since sympathy and empathy are not the same thing. I believe we should capture some salient points about the difference between the two.

For me, sympathy is a form of communication that does not necessarily address the underlying issues. Imagine that you are walking past a friend in the company parking garage whose car has run out of gas. A sympathetic response would be, "gee that's really tough luck. That happened to me once and it was a real pain," and then you walk away without considering offering any form of assistance. An empathetic response would be something along the lines of: "gee that's really inconvenient for you. Why don't I try phoning my auto club to see if we can get some gas delivered?"

Transparent management and leadership is one of the worst forms of sympathy. Management, at all levels, is about leadership and the ability to translate strategy into meaningful actions to one's team. Not being accountable for the organization's actions is clearly sympathy with the employees that achieves no higher purpose, and can actually destroy the core fabric of the organization. Beware of the sympathizing managers, who make you feel short term happiness with no concrete results. They are great if you have a personal problem, but will never be able to help you out with organizational issues, which proves that they are either helpless sympathizers, or clueless sympathizers, with no idea what your real needs are.

HELPLESS SYMPATHIZERS

Helpless sympathizers are leaders that may mean well, but they are torn between being popular with their employees and salvaging what they see as the best of a bad situation. Sympathy applies to business as well as people leadership. I vividly recall my first years as a researcher. At that time I felt my contribution was under-rated and that I deserved a promotion to recognize my accomplishments. I was responsible for a highly technical part of a "strategic" project, building signal processing capabilities for packet telephony (in 1992 this was pretty pioneering work). My manager and his manager agreed with the assessment that this was critical and deserved a promotion, yet for two years I received no recognition or reward. Those were the days of annual or legacy recognition. So, waiting for a whole year to be told that my management was supportive of a promotion, yet my director was not, pissed me off. My director felt that until we delivered the final product, the topic of recognition should not be discussed. I was naively happy that my management supported me and felt that it was simply unfortunate that the senior leadership did not agree with us.

After two years, and major delays to our overall research and development program, we were no closer to completion. Needless to say, I was very frustrated. It seemed that the date for the much awaited recognition would never come. So, I started looking for another job. I have to be clear the technical work was challenging and the people were great, however the overall environment was not rewarding. Maybe that is a subject for another book one day on why a technology challenging environment is necessary, but not sufficient for a technologist.

At that time, Bell Northern Research was part of the tri-corporate structure with Bell Canada and Nortel Networks. Even then my move to Nortel Networks was formally blocked for almost a year. Human Resources said there was not much they could do, and that it was all in my director's hands. To their credit, they offered me loads of useless sympathetic support.

Only when I received an external employment offer from Ericsson Corporation was my internal move to another division approved (a six-month transition period was requested – ridiculous). It was then that I made myself a promise, that when I got promoted to management ranks, if I truly believed in one of my team's ability to be promoted, then it would be my success or failure to make it happen. Sympathizers ensure that you keep your problems your own, rather than assuming them as a true leader and making your challenges theirs as true leaders. If they think you are fine where you are, they should tell you. Passing the buck is an abdication of responsibility.

CLUELESS SYMPATHIZERS

Clueless sympathizers tend to be pretty smart individuals who know a little about a lot of things. They tend to have a high IQ with respectively lower applied intelligence (more to come on this topic). These individuals are good at emotional manipulation. In my personal experience, they know the value of a person and relate well to the issues, but cannot see how to move things forward, or they really believe that sympathy will carry the day. You get from them two things: great "ears" and you feel good about yourself or "greater ears" and you get requests to provide them with additional information.

Do they really get it? If someone does not get it, then clarifications and requests for more analysis are the kiss of death. How many times have delays due to lack of ability to make decisions come back to haunt an organization? Clueless sympathizers know what is important, but they cannot make the decision or trust their people. It's a bit of arrogance on their part to conclude that "if we don't get it, then it can't be the way forward." I have to admit there are cases when communication is blurred. Engineers are just as guilty as others; they tend to capture the value of their engineering recommendations in terms of technology requirements, sometimes missing the mark on business value. Sometimes the best technical solution is not the optimal business solution, be it in long-term relationships or partnerships with suppliers.

In short, what I am trying to say is beware of leaders who make you feel stupid rather than invest in educating you about what they are trying to do.

I am personally guilty of bad communication on many occasions. I recall when I first got promoted to Director and my manager was Barbara Callaghan, then VP Business Operation for Nortel's Data Networks Division. Barbara's background was finance. I had, at the time, what I believed was a brilliant idea, and one that required her support and additional funding. She asked me, "Why would our clients care?" I was shocked. All my life my previous managers had been individuals like myself that had moved up the technology ranks, so when she honestly told me she did not get it, I was at a loss, I was frustrated and felt that I had a clueless boss. Let me tell you how wrong I was.

When Barb asked me why our clients would care, you would have had to feel for me since for the past six years or so I had always communicated my ideas in technical terms. I learned my lesson fast that she viewed me as a business leader in charge of a technical team, another important turning point in my career. Thanks Barb.

Back to the brilliant idea, and yes bragging does bring some comfort. Like most of our competitors at the time – namely Cisco – we had marketing conferences, and I felt there was a need for client planning workshops, which basically amounted to empathetic forums where we would share how the technology works, rather than simply share the technology and the technology roadmap.

I restated my idea using terms of customer satisfaction and potential of increased revenue for our new products and features. That sparked the launch of the Network Planners Workshop (NPW), an industry-first conference where Nortel engineers and clients spent time working through scenarios to apply the technology. What was unique was that traditional customer workshops focused on one-way communication – by the manufacturer to their client base about features and capabilities, and rarely a meaningful exchange on how to use the products. The data switching customers loved the dialogue and I have to say it was a huge success. I believe the NPW was the ultimate in empathy between supplier and customer. Many thanks to Anne Raymond, my partner in crime, and someone who believed in me and what we were doing. Without her, I doubt we would have had the success we did.

SUMMARY

My task in this chapter was not to explain the difference between empathy and sympathy. It was about being able to relate to a certain situation and the individuals involved and how important that is for leadership.

Empathy is clearly a lost art these days. Most successful leaders are ones who exhibit various forms of empathy, and who do not confuse empathy with sympathy. The question of true empathy or fake is irrelevant for this discussion. You will face a lot of sympathizers; the key is to work around them and realize they are humouring you at best (be it genuine or malicious sympathy). You make your own destiny, so get going.

Empathy is critical for you as a leader, as a subordinate and as a communicator. Communication is about relating, and assuming people are not capable of understanding is a key failing point in communications. When someone claims they understand and support you, they should be able to produce results to help you get on with your endeavours. If not, it's useless sympathy.

So if you get a lot of ear and no action, your manager is a first-class wanker.

If you are told this is the way it is with no explanation, your manager is an even bigger wanker.

If you want to communicate, think of your audience and their ability to comprehend. If you don't, you won't be a particularly good communicator, but you will be an outstanding wanker.

CHAPTER 4

Is the vehicle more important than the destination?

I AM A FIRM BELIEVER that people should know how they contribute to the bottom line, especially those taking part in transformational projects. This chapter is written in the context of the massive transformational projects that corporations are frequently forced to undertake in response to any number of stimuli, but most often changes in technology and services, or in enabling a related cultural shift.

I find these projects tend to take on a life of their own and few of the people involved know the end objective, or if they do, they neglect to routinely revisit the original business case to ensure they are still on track to meet those objectives. People get so busy delivering the business transformation tools and solving related problems that they lose track of what it is they are trying to transform and why. Lots of intelligent people set up five-year plus transformational projects, particularly in the technology field where physical and system infrastructure was to be upgraded. Many of these projects were at risk of failure from the outset. I can safely say, when the delivery is five or more years out, more often than not these projects will be over budget, behind schedule and offer little in terms of future benefits. It is critical to have concrete short terms goals or else the transformation will yield what was best in class five years earlier. With business models changing through technology every few years, this would be a waste of money and corporate effort.

HINDSIGHT IS 20:20

I have a simple theory: when the length of a project exceeds the change in enabling technology, or the business models change faster than the time required to deliver the new system, the project will most likely fail unless the changing dynamics are taken into consideration. For example, let's assume you are building a plane, and that the entire process takes five years from initial design to first flight. If key components, such as the fuselage, evolve every two years, then by the time the plane is finished, you are using fuselage material that is two to three years old – pretty lousy for a plane that is yet to fly. So either you need to start delivering planes every two years, or design the fuselage in the last two years of the plane's development. In other words, when the speed with which people deliver on their projects is slower than the speed with which the technologies, requirements and services change, you have a vicious circle. What is needed is a framework and consistent tracking of business objectives, complete with interim practical deliverables to accommodate changes that inevitably arise.

Increasingly, one of the most common delays in large projects is too much reliance upon governance to make decisions and solve problems. "Time to deliver" is a metric that should never be ignored. I know governance is a hot topic these days, as indicated by the emergence of companies specializing in governance and governance textbooks and governance tools. But as important as governance is, too much of it can be an indication that the leader is willing to be rendered inert by constantly consulting with various stakeholders (a time and money consuming process) rather than making intelligent recommendations in order to keep moving forward. This is another example of the vehicle becoming more important than the destination. Incidentally, there are numerous traditional definitions of governance. Basically, governance is intended to ensure the relevant stakeholders buy into the project and is informed at all stages of development. Used right, governance is a great tool, but when the process is humoured for the sake of implementing the process, it becomes a rubber stamping technique or governance through democracy. I would like to point out that good leadership mandates decision making and gathering multiple data points, but not necessarily voting on next steps.

When major projects fail, leaders tend to blame the people they want to get rid of or they blame related tools and processes. And now it seems that governance is the latest in an abused mosaic of tools and processes. I know this is tangential, but I have seen so many examples of this behaviour it is another abuse of the vehicle. Is governance another measure for justifying bad leadership? Or is governance meant to ensure all stakeholders are informed? Better yet, is governance a set of tools to make something successful?

But what is governance really? Or more importantly, what should governance be? My view is that governance should be the vehicle to secure an appropriate level of buy-in and alignment of an entire leadership team. If properly utilized, governance would then reduce the chances of lamenting in hindsight many years later about what could have gone right. Governance, done right, is a great tool to keep a multi-disciplinary project focused on the underlying business objectives and metrics. Governance, done wrong, often results in the project taking on a life of its own.

Let me put it another way. If people treated the corporation's dollars and resources as their own, they would never allow these circumstances to occur. I believe this also applies to leaders that lose their own businesses, not in the same way; the questions become for them when to cut their losses and move on. Would one live in a house where they work on fixing a leaking roof for many years? When personal fortunes suffer, an individual's practical governance mechanisms take over before things get driven further into the ground. Swift surgical cutting and revising objectives typically offer better outcomes than slow painful bleeding.

There are rarely quick fixes for complex issues. One thing I would recommend would be designing a framework with short-term deliverables instead of a project with a three to five year life to deliver on its promise. A framework enables the flexibility of implementation and keeps the business metrics as the main focus. Governance at multiple levels – financial, technical, business value – will provide the right level of attention, however, success in the transformation game is ultimately determined by leadership and oversight, particularly since not everyone involved or affected by transformation is happy about it. I always say that leadership is not a democracy.

Human beings, by nature, resist fundamental change, be it cultural change or business process change, meaning that transformation projects don't get the buy-in of everyone. As a result, you often need to undertake a slightly more dictatorial leadership style and actually force behaviour modification in order to invoke necessary and dramatic change. The more dramatic the change required, the more dictatorial the hand that is required to police and guide it. Leadership is not about popularity, but at the same time, leaders should not be blind, nor believe they are always right or, more importantly, that a good idea will find its way without the practical aspects of implementation being well thought out.

Another example here was the multiple rounds of layoffs that were experienced at Nortel, the intent of which was to optimize the workforce for the business. The formula was academic and the execution never customized. The end result was rounds of layoffs to adhere to a specific formula with no applied business metrics; simple cosmetic changes that fooled no one but the corporation. The fundamental metric of specific business profitability was not translated to each business unit or division. The end result was a lot of leaders refusing to comply, with their focus on saving the business rather than adhering to some formula.

I would like to share an additional thought with you. When we embark on projects and design their governance and reporting, we assume things will go according to plan. We never question if the processes we have in place will be optimal when things go off the rails. I am a firm believer that different leadership styles and characteristics and tools are required for different predicaments. The leadership required to chart new territory differs from the leadership to maintain business as usual, and both differ from the leadership required when times are bad.

There are three characteristics of bad leadership in the context of transformational projects:

1   The ones with the attitude that everyone around is stupid, and that they don't actually "get it." Rule of thumb: anyone who thinks they are the smartest person they know is neither blessed, nor realistic.

2   We will make it work at any cost. There is no doubt in my mind that with the right amount of money and effort we can send a submarine to the moon, but is that the optimal vehicle or way to get to the moon?

3   We are almost there! Seeing the light at the end of the tunnel is great, but when it is totally dark, the light reaches from very faraway places. Some people never give up and are always optimistic, both commendable characteristics, but it is critical to recognize when to write something off. In some of the projects I was involved in, the end was heralded as two years or more away. Amazingly, the end never came. It was always two years away. Again, business benefits should be the only guide; any other measure of progress is irrelevant. No matter how fast you go on a stationary bicycle you will remain in the same spot, so marks for efforts that yield no results matter only in kindergarten.

SHOULD THE GARDENER DETERMINE WHICH NEIGHBOURHOOD YOU LIVE IN?

When we embark on a transformational project, like everything in life, we want the best affordable solution. In the technology realm we select the newest technology, we pick best in class enabling products, and we leverage the latest processes. Theoretically this is an optimal start. I would do the same, however, one thing we rarely do a good job of is predicting or quantifying the end-to-end system performance; we assume the vision and the architecture and pray that the partners and stakeholders will take care of the execution.

Normally after the strategy is set and the high level structure is established, the various pieces are farmed out to their respective silos where they are optimized in relative isolation. Groups of people working on disparate parts of a transformation project need to see and talk to each other. Good people tend to optimize their areas of responsibility and, without the benefit of the big picture, the result may be a suboptimal end-to-end system. Very tough to build the fastest car and the most fuel efficient car at the same time, especially if the teams don't talk to each other!

You'll note that the name of this chapter makes reference to a gardener. I have to point out here I have nothing but the utmost respect for the folks that work the earth. I am alluding to the importance of the role of a gardener in the overall home ownership equation. The gardener is someone who is no doubt important, but not so much as to really be a deciding factor for which house to purchase. Gardeners tend to service specific areas of a city, so if the decision is to change houses or location, I doubt we would consider gardening services to be a deciding factor on where we should move to. In transformational projects, we sometime let our emotions turn into something analogous to the gardener in the home location decision, when what we really need to be doing is to select anchor points in the transformation that pertain to cost and benefits rather than superfluous issues. But, as we are human, we allow emotions or other comparatively unimportant factors to have an effect on what and how we do things.

So when we start transformation projects, we often pick pieces and vendors that, as time progresses, are no longer complementary. At that point we have to ask, did we pick the right anchor points? The reality is, through vendor consolidation, partners become competitors and you can see their widening rift during the project. The length of the project could have caused a divergence in vendor objectives or the changing underlying technologies could have shifted. Regardless, the owners of the transformational project should make the decision on the anchor elements based on sound long-term rationale, not emotions, old business allegiances, friendships or personal preferences. As things change, not all pieces can carry the same level of importance, and flexibility and frameworks are the key to success. A well designed framework will clearly highlight the important anchor pieces that a project should rally around. Rather than riding out the initial investment in resources and funds, one can quickly assess what is important. I know, people rarely like to say they are wrong or have wasted corporate resources, but biting the bullet early is a sign of true leadership when things do not work.

A word about frameworks, I find well defined frameworks synonymous with ecosystems, in which there is inherent flexibility that allows for adjustment and changes. One dictionary definition of ecosystem that I particularly like is: "a system formed by the interaction of a community of organisms with their physical environment."

On a practical level, a framework defines the overall design, and also defines how the various components interact with each other. A proper framework also defines the book ends and the anchor points. Building bridges requires proper framework design and analysis. What is the objective of the bridge; what will the bridge look like, and what is the material that will be used? Sometimes, we are so smart we decide on all three aspects at once. That may be good when cooking a stew but not terribly smart when building a bridge. A familiar example is the car stereo of the early 80's. In the old days you had balance, fade, treble and bass. Then manufacturers started dazzling us with the various features that could be controlled on a radio. I recall in the 1980's, Honda and other Japanese car manufacturers thought more audio options in a car stereo would be a selling feature that North American cars did not have. Some car stereo systems had seven fields and knobs you could adjust. I contend that unless one was an audiophile, adjusting seven factors to listen to music usually yielded a sub-optimal listening experience. So either try things out, go with the default setting, or accept the delays that will occur for you to learn how to operate the radio. When you have numerous moving pieces, decide what you want to move or modify with a firm plan in mind. Just because something is the latest innovation in a field does not necessarily mean it will work for you from the start. Basically do not assume things will always work as planned.

In every transformational project, one should select a few anchor partners. One should decide who they should hitch their wagon to. That usually stems from who is best able to deliver business value. What I find in these projects is that the original cast of suppliers stays the same throughout the life of the project(s); and more often they are not aligned with their individual offerings. In a lot of cases, one vendor or anchor point overlaps the other and gets into their space. When that happens, it becomes important to decide who you are going to stick with.

My point is to pick your anchor suppliers and partners carefully. In other words, do not let the skills of the gardener determine which house you buy. I have yet to see anyone change their house because of the gardeners serving the area. In numerous cases, the light at the end of the tunnel mentality causes one of the anchor partners to drag you down. For example in the IT systems space assume you select Amdocs for a billing system and Telcordia as an inventory system, which are both great vendors in their space. That would have been fine before 2008. In 2008, Amdocs purchased an inventory system themselves and their efforts are now to integrate seamlessly between billing and inventory systems. I am sure that their corporate strategy – gaining market share and mindshare – was the main motivation, rather than easing the pain of folks who chose their billing system. This puts Telcordia in an awkward position and keeping both "anchor" points without clear delineation between them or without having added any custom development will cause nothing but grief, and a practical roadmap and architecture with interfaces becomes a must. Or, what happens is the transformation becomes inefficient and the total cost of ownership shoots through the roof.

One thing becomes clear. As tension mounts between the various "partners, we are no longer on solid foundations, unless we have a well-established framework and definition for what is the expected role between each partner. Solid foundation is the key phrase. As the individual foundational pieces get re-aligned, one should question how solid the mix is. I doubt anyone would disagree that building skyscrapers in Venice would be a risky endeavour. The tallest building in the world incidentally is in Dubai right in the desert. No doubt ensuring the right foundation was a critical step before embarking on the project.

LIFE OF ITS OWN

An amazing phenomenon happens with long projects. New hires are often added throughout the life of a multi-year project. These resource additions, knowing no better, believe that the transformation project is a product or a service. Few of them grasp the fact they are working on an enabling suite of tools and processes to support the business. The more frequent the overall delays, the less time spent on educating individuals how they contribute to the bottom line, at which point the vehicle truly becomes the destination for a large number of people.

In addition, I contend that in three years, more than 50 per cent of the leadership teams on the delivery and stakeholder side will change, be it from fatigue or frustration. What was then supposed to be the corporate saviour and the new way of life becomes the albatross around the corporate neck. People start rolling their eyes at the mention of the transformation project and wish the pain would just end.

Nothing is more difficult than admitting ones mistakes, however, the sooner the better.

LEGACY AND ACADEMICS – THE KISS OF DEATH

Greenfield opportunities, just like monopoly situations, are wonderful, and those of us who have experienced either are among the fortunate few. I define transformations as the replacement of existing systems and processes to invoke a meaningful change in how the business operates. If otherwise, the effort can't be described as transformational. So when an organization embarks on a transformational effort, something pretty fundamental, the best strategic minds are allocated or hired to help out with these transformational endeavours. Their strategic talent can be listed in three categories:

1   **Practical Leaders** – The people who understand the business and its present and future requirements and are capable of a developing a practical long-term plan that can be executed upon. They take into consideration that things will go wrong but can accommodate changes in style and leadership.

2   **Academic Leaders** – The people who understand the business and its present and future requirements, but have no clue how to operationalize their vision, and who have never done any delivery type of work in their careers. Academic leaders tend to see everything as a Greenfield opportunity, not understanding how

to migrate from their current situation. Most consultants fall into this category – very intelligent people that have rarely had practical experiences. (For what it's worth, some of my best friends are consultants.)

3 **Legacy Leaders** – The people who are not strategic but have a proven record for delivery. Barry Baptie, who I greatly admire, was a senior executive at TELUS, described this kind of leader as one who excels in "paving the cow paths." They will build on their experience and end up using the latest technology to create a legacy implementation. The erosion of telephony for most telecommunications services providers presents a good example, in which a number of service providers ended up building next generation systems to deal with the changing revenue models and leverage web services. What they ended up with was replicating their old systems with new technology – basically sinking investment for a declining revenue stream, while fitting new services and products into the "old" way at great expense. In cases like these, I can only hope that the leadership team doesn't repeat the mistake in the transformation required to fix the transformation.

Every person has a little of each of the above characteristics, and a healthy mix is not bad. Usually you have more of numbers two and three, resulting in a drawn-out multi-year, behind schedule, de-scoped project.

I believe that the more fundamental question that needs to be answered first is: what about legacy systems and processes? You cannot build a new car engine without questioning the car itself and the supporting elements. If the new engine is also meant to "operate" the old car then believe me it will look a lot like the old engine. Using new components to build old systems is not terribly transformational. I cover this in a bit more detail and with examples in the next section.

Simply put, *using c++ to write FORTRAN is not the most effective use of object oriented code.* I say FORTRAN is the best programming language to write FORTRAN. I get grief from my non-technical colleagues and corporate communications folks for using technical terms that are difficult for some people to understand. I tell them that I am not trying to cater only to the geeks, just that most of my experiences are technology related. If you are a technologist, hopefully the statement concerning FORTRAN is profound to you. For others, what I am trying to say is that it is unwise to buy new tools to use them the same way. A Swiss army knife has many usages when one needs a compact all-in-one gadget, however I do not see many wine servers using a Swiss army knife instead of a cork screw for opening bottles. Gut feel, not an optimal strategy.

One of the objectives of this section is to provide some tips about undertaking transformational projects, and to suggest some questions that you should regularly ask yourself about measurable data points throughout the project, particularly in the common instances when transformational projects have heavy technology dependencies. The difference between great success and dismal failure can be very small. Success or failure depends upon the ability of the transformation project to deal with the new business models. I would venture that even when two projects look the same, and the actual people involved are equally dedicated, it is only when end results are compared after a long period of time that one can assess success or failure. Nortel is another good example here. Their plans for investments for new products and areas were comparable to their peers, however, as time has proved, they fell short of transforming the corporation into a viable entity.

Another case in point is Microsoft. I believe Bill Gates tried to sell the concept of Windows to IBM, but later succeeded in making Windows the de-facto operating system for the personal computer. IBM weathered the storm and re-invented itself. Who could have predicted the change and evolution of Facebook five years ago, or Google ten years ago? Conversely, who could have predicted that Nortel would go bankrupt ten years ago?

In an ever changing climate, the design and architecture should ensure the business benefit can always be measured and tracked. An invaluable tip is to ensure that the architecture takes into account the varying rates of evolution of the individual pieces. To elaborate, if you are designing a system with two pieces whose underlying usage and life cycle and technology evolution are different, then do not hard connect them. IMS (IP Multimedia Subsystem) was heralded in the early 2000s as the next generation transformation for mobile operators. Like most evolutions, it was vendor/supplier driven and the service providers rallied around that at a later date. A lot of work was done on IMS to define a transformational framework, and the service to validate the framework was telephony. At that time wireless data was in its infancy. So 10 years of work in the standards bodies was done where the applicable service was voice communications. The year is now 2011 and the dominant services are applications and data connectivity for mobile operators. To make a long story short, few operators have implemented IMS as their biggest issue was IP connectivity and the explosion of IP traffic. IMS did a brilliant job in defining the various interfaces between the components of a wireless core, the IP transport network and the IT systems. The goodness of IMS is for its framework. Few providers implemented IMS fully as voice communication is not so important today. So when the IMS push started they should have decoupled explicitly the voice linkages. That has happened now and the IMS framework is being implemented with its interface and components as a transformational effort, I would say 12 to13 years after the inception. This is an example of salvaging a transformational effort that initially hard connected the pieces. Since voice was the only service when IMS started, they never predicted the need to validate for other services.

SUMMARY

When building a complex system with numerous moving pieces, if one piece changes in technology every two years and the other changes every five, then to keep the overall system up to date you will have to build everything every two years rather than simply change the piece with the two-year life span. The same concept applies if the delivery times also have a wide variance. In addition, are we building new enabling tools for new products and services, or for the old suite of products and services? I know these two statements sound intuitive, perhaps even patronizing, however I believe that most of the projects that go on endlessly are ones in which this fundamental error has been made. Do not deliver today what was great five years ago or, gut feel, you will need to do the project again, hopefully with better guidance and results the second time around.

Finally, if I leave you with only one thing, never forget that transformation is a way of life, and not a single project in time. If you look at the companies with successful track records, transformation is just part of the ongoing way they do business. IBM and Google fit the bill here, as both have been in a perpetual state of evolution ever since their inception. When I started my engineering career, IBM was a PC powerhouse that prided itself on great innovations in hardware. Today IBM has sold its PC business (LENOVO) but maintains its core hardware skills to benefit its server business and licences innovations to others. They realized that just because they are good at certain things does not mean they should do everything themselves. Google, likewise, is interested only in your identity as a user so they can leverage that relationship with advertisers. I would say they are the largest advertising firm in the world. Their business model allows them to offer free email and telephony to ensure they keep you as a user while they make their money through selling "eyeballs," a business model that has marginalized numerous telecommunication services.

So if you join a project in its third year and the project was supposed to deliver benefits a year earlier, the project is a wanker.

If you join a project in which no one can explain to you the benefits of the overall project beyond your component, the project is really a wanker.

And if you join a project where you are told you are not smart enough to understand the big picture, the project is a wanker; its leader is a wanker, and you are a wanker for agreeing to stay.

> *"Sometimes a mistake is like wearing white after Labour Day, and sometimes a mistake is invading Russia in winter!"*
> — ALAN BURNSIDE

CHAPTER 5

Lost in translation

STRATEGY IS CRITICAL in all organizations, and people at all levels need to know where they are in an organization and where the organization itself is going. Strategists, like the term suggests, are big thinkers, but big ideas need to be translated into actionable components. Strategists fall into two categories: people who can think but cannot execute, and people who can do both (the latter kind are a rare breed). Once a strategy is nailed, it is important to translate it into a project and ensure all aspects of that strategy are sorted out.

ARCHITECTS — A MISUSED ENTITY

When an organization translates strategy into an action plan, the work is often split into various components of work or projects, thus requiring numerous hand-offs. The larger the organization, the more hand-offs there are, and the greater the potential loss of details. I believe to avoid the loss of ideas and benefits from strategy to execution, you need a team of unique individuals who can straddle both the strategy and practical realms to ensure the strategy is properly translated into actions.

Let's look at the realities of a large organization. Most top-down strategies tend to become edicts, and if no one translates these edicts into coherent steps, people will deliver the edicts or new programs the old way – a recurring theme. This is simply human nature. The folks in the trenches are busy with day-to-day operations and problem solving and often perceive these edicts as added overhead and people meddling in their jobs with no clue to the actual effort required to deliver. It becomes critical to share with them why the longer term vision needs a defined reality today or it will never happen in a timely fashion.

This delicate role of translating a vision into something realizable is best dealt with by someone I call an architect. Civil engineers can build anything you want, but the architects are the ones that know what the living experience and usage of that structure will look like. The task of architecting is the critical element in this equation. Someone needs to always articulate how something will be used and the desired user experience, and that is the role of the architect. Ensure that the "architecting" or system analysis happens and the benefits articulated. Fair thought process is one way to ensure all stakeholders are informed and are part of the solution.

THE ENEMY WITHIN...

It is not malicious behaviour when people resist change or a new mode of operations. Usually explicitly malicious people are let go. I know, I am back to the same theme of people that do things their way and at all levels tend to understand the new concepts, and when they cannot, they ignore them by putting up invisible roadblocks. Thus, governance is of extreme importance; not dictatorial governance by issuing a new structure and process, but proper buy-in governance at all levels, and more importantly, explaining and touching all aspects of a new process or structure or technology.

I recall when Jules Meunier introduced the Portfolio Management Team (PMT) concept for the product teams at Nortel. We had weekly management meetings and the whole leadership team was dedicated to following through on every detail on how to make the new process work. He was personally present at all weekly meetings to ensure proper execution of the new PMT governance process. It was success-ful to the extent that all Nortel business units adopted it. Without the rigour that our division put in place (yes, thanks Jules for personally overseeing everything), the other business units did not realize the benefits we enjoyed. Simply forcing the PMT structure did not yield the same results that our division had on execution and the success of governance and matrix reporting (pretty novel in the late 90's). It was another instance of the vehicle being more important than the desti-nation. The various divisions added the required overhead for the PMT process without forcing the new behaviour, which basically made them less efficient and increased their overhead. Our division had invested the time and resources in architecting how to deploy the PMT process. The other divisions implemented the process without the benefit of architecting it. This is the equivalent of an engineer building some-thing by just taking a look at it, or building a bridge because you have used one.

The people involved in such situations are basically good at the core, but their leaders have to have the stamina and all the individuals required to guide all levels of the organization and to see how the new structure will work. Leaders cannot simply provide a magical formula and hope it will work. They have to personally live it and oversee it and, more importantly, care about the success and metrics. You need archi-tects to guide novel thought and ideas.

On a side note is my experience at a parent-teacher association (PTA) meeting. When I bought my first house in Ottawa I was shocked that I was charged an educational tax, and being the rational person I am, I phoned the City of Ottawa taxation department and complained that there was an error in my tax assessment as I have no kids and should not be charged for an educational tax. After the city employees stopped laughing, they indicated that it is applied to all homeowners and I should think of it as an investment in our collective future. This made a lot of sense to me. I followed up by asking how I could go about being more involved, and their response was possibly attend a PTA meeting to see how the educational curriculum gets decided on and the funding spent. To make a long story short, I attended a PTA meeting and was surprised at how many parents voiced their expertise in the level of difficulty of a certain subject. I requested the floor and asked all these parents about what qualified them to make the judgement call that Grade 10 math was too difficult. Shockingly their response was "we took Grade 10 math 20 years ago." I did voice my concern that this was the least applicable reason for them to make a call. Alas it fell on deaf ears, one of the few misapplications of democracy I believe.

On another side note, the PMT structure and process was way ahead of its time and now organizations are implementing the milder flavour of PMT through governance and fair thought processes.

And yes, there are always a few resistors (I would not use the term bad apples) that need to be let go. The sooner we come to that conclusion, the better it is for the organization and the people themselves.

CUSTOM PERHAPS, BUT DEFINITELY STRATEGIC!

"In theory there's no difference between theory and practice. In practice there is."
— YOGI BERRA

I believe that the term "strategic" project, or "strategic" effort or transformation, is terribly abused.

In my view, strategic effort is transformational effort. However, it seems that all work that cannot be justified as part of standard business operations is usually called "strategic" so that it can be allowed to happen. The reasons are many, but we tend to use the "strategic" label for projects that are custom in nature or those with questionable or uncertain financial assessments; both can be coined easily with the right data. Regardless of the validity of the reasoning, when you have too many strategic projects which are basically "custom" or "special," you need to be organized to handle such work.

Beware when all effort is focused on proving new products, customer segments or solutions, unless the entire organization is structured around rendering custom solutions with no foresight to mass produce or replicate procedures or products. As a side note, even corporations whose business is designing custom solutions – such as IBM Global Services – work on replicating some solutions and leveraging certain processes. If all the work is earmarked as strategic, the question becomes: who is delivering on what is needed to keep the organization going and the lights on, and how are these projects leveraged for the betterment of the whole organization?

All corporations should undertake strategic efforts that will deliver continued differentiation, new capabilities, new customer segments and increased profitability, but when the bulk of operational activity is deemed to be strategic, it means that something else is being neglected. Not only that, but when the bulk of the business is strategic, or "custom," ask yourself if you are organized to do that effectively. Strategic projects, because they are transformational, tend to be "firsts," hence they become custom built by default.

I should say here that some companies have been successful in organizing themselves to specialize in offering custom solutions. Again, IBM Global Services is a great example of an organization that was built specifically to deliver custom solutions, but it's a bit of an exceptional case. Imagine, for example, what would happen to Ford if the company suddenly became solely consumed with a strategic projects like building the perfect electric car or expanding its racing division that it began to compromise on continuing new innovation for key products like the Mustang and F150 pick-up truck?

Not only that, but when companies are hungry to demonstrate a new capability or to prove new strategic ideas or products, they typically offer them at reduced margins or a loss to win the business. The plan to get people to try the products and services tends to result in organizations abandoning the appropriate profit/loss assessments. The hope is always that at some point in time they will "upsell" standard services, or that this will be an introductory one-off activity. Alas, that is rarely the case. Note that the Apple iPad is an exception to this rule.

But, there is no denying the sex appeal of strategic achievements. There is however, a difference between conquering Greenland and Australia. Both are comparable in size, but one is potentially more attractive and economically important than the other. Team members and their leaders need to ensure the investments in strategic projects make sense, and have the potential to result in recurring net revenue.

In addition to the sex appeal of a strategic win, there is the beauty and satisfaction of successful execution. The top experts from all parts of the organization work together to make it happen as companies tend to put their best and brightest on strategic projects. I can tell you, as someone who has participated on these teams, it is extremely fulfilling on all levels. Your knowledge is stretched with people who are good in their own right, and more importantly, the project tends to be on the minds of the senior executives all the time, so the rewards are reflective of that. It is no surprise that individuals working on strategic projects are rewarded anywhere from 30 per cent to 100 per cent more than others who are doing their job on "non-strategic" work.

At the same time, we have two fundamental problems when strategic projects become the predominant business activity in an organization that is designed around delivering mass repeatable products and services.

1 Strategic projects require strategic thinkers and execution professionals and those are a rare high priced commodity. No organization has enough superstars to accommodate multiple strategic initiatives. The result is invariably that you end up stretching the good employees, or promoting a few academic pretenders or "butchers" that simply add overhead.

2   Whenever something is done strategically, the question should always be: can it be repeated? Repeatability is not usually the main concern with strategic projects, so the organization as a whole does not benefit from the learned lesson unless the project was built as an enabling project. We all know things rarely go as planned when one is doing something new. So, effectively everything is a first. Beautiful, but how does it move the whole organization forward? The answer is that they rarely do, the reason being that nothing becomes ingrained in the corporate culture and processes, which is unfortunate.

These two behaviours result in an indirect tragedy; most of the corporate oversight and effort is wasted on "strategic" low margin business. New products and services need to be profitable in the short term as well as over time. How I hate the words "get in now and up-sell later." Clients are not stupid. They see through that and will continuously negotiate contracts competitively down. I personally always assume a declining cost of goods over time.

NO FARM TEAM

Our TELUS CEO, Darren Entwistle, reminds us relentlessly of the importance of replenishing our critical resources and scarce skills. How true. Not doing so presents long term negative impacts to which corporations don't pay enough attention. These are the up-and-comers, the "farm teams" of expertise, and the "how-to-build-the-next-generation" experts. How many times do we joke and say that it is always the same five people who do most of the work? Basically we have come to accept bad planning in this area as a corporate reality. I was just as guilty as the next person, always using the same resources (that I considered reliable and trustworthy) for projects that were deemed important. But if we never put a structure around these strategic projects, be they for revenue or enabling purposes, we will never holistically benefit from them in growing the talent of the organization and, more importantly, balancing the work load. If a strategic project is meant to launch a new business, then we need to ensure we bring up the whole organization to understand what will be delivered, so the organization and the employees can scale with the strategy. So if we over burden our senior employees with work, they will not have the time or energy to mentor the junior employees, thereby creating a future talent vacuum.

When an organization is constantly busied with strategic projects, it sends a clear message to the employees that such projects are the only important ones. The same people (the seasoned employees with a delivery track record) tend to be involved in them all the time, sending a negative message to the bulk of the employees. There is no rule of thumb about how many strategic projects are enough or too many. I say that you should be able to count strategic projects on one hand. If these projects are done as one-offs, then there are no larger benefits to the organization and junior people are usually excluded, which is demoralizing for most of the employees, and in particular for the excited and energetic young recruits. Thinking that they are going nowhere fast, the new and emerging talent at the organization will tend to leave in frustration, reinforcing a shortage of talented resources that are critical to future success.

At TELUS, we have a number of programs meant to promote and develop young graduates, who are a joy to work with and tend to provide innovative ideas. They tend to get a flavour for the whole business in different roles and interact with all kinds of people. We can learn a lot from them. My favourite example is the introduction of social networking. People like me felt we had to use these communication media and I still struggle with how to best leverage them. For the longest time I used a blog as I would use email. But our young recruits grew up with social networking and they take to it like fish to water. Fortunately, they are not shy about educating old dogs like me.

LEGACY PROCESSES

On these "strategic" projects, time is of the essence and the majority of the team members are pretty senior, hence no real effort is made to ensure that next generation processes or employees are developed or implemented. Not to mention, when you have a bunch of superstars, they all tend to think they are right and therefore best suited to lead.

Back to a common theme: no matter how senior a person is, they go with what and who they know. It is a rare breed of individuals that make the time to invest in finding out what is appropriate for new technologies, products and services. How many companies built new technologies the same old way and wondered why they could not realize the benefits of the new technology (reduced cost of ownership and faster time to market)?

SUMMARY

When you are involved in a large project, you should ensure all aspects are addressed from strategy to architecture, to design, to implementation, to deployment. New enabling technologies should define new products and services at all levels. Architecture is not just a strategy role; it is at all levels of adoption. When you are in a leadership position, it may stretch your personal limits to oversee all aspects, so hire and recruit the right talent to support you in all the required areas. Out of all the functions, architecture is the one that tends to be "assumed" or misinterpreted. So hire the architects who share your objectives and can articulate the end-to-end requirements to succeed. Architects are a special breed of people who require unique handling. They enjoy change and have the required track record to translate new ideas and strategies into concrete action plans. A word of caution, do not bury them in pure strategy or pure tactical work, or you will lose their unique skill set and capabilities.

If you are a senior and, hopefully, empowered person in your organization, question the viability and utilization of strategic projects. Ensure the benefits are holistic rather than merely serving to dig the organization deeper into the legacy way of doing things. Always think of how you would ensure that the future superstars do not become apathetic or leave the organization in frustration. Nothing draws a more pathetic picture for an organization than when all the experts are due to retire in a few years, and having been so busy delivering on strategic projects, they forgot to pass on their knowledge and ability to help younger generations.

Lastly, the financial burden of badly executed strategic projects is long lasting and needs to be stemmed as soon as possible.

Strategy, unlike a Harrier jet, cannot function with only two data points, the 100,000 foot view and the one foot view as end points. Someone has to map out the trajectory, or the strategy is a wanker

Strategy is not only about building something, it is about operationalizing it and ensuring the benefits are fully realized. If not, this strategy too is a wanker.

An architect should understand the benefits as well as the actual implementation of a project. If otherwise, the architect is a wanker.

If you are told something is strategic, ask yourself, how that will transform into business as usual? If it is clear that it won't, then the project is a wanker.

If everyone is busy with strategic projects, and new talent isn't being developed, the company is a wanker; its leaders are wankers, and the people who continue to work in such an environment are wankers for not leaving.

And if it is the same group of people always working on strategic projects, believe me the organization will deplete its scarce resources and fatigue the cherished few, making wankers out of everybody.

Lastly, if an organization does not invest in its new blood and create a sustainable farm team, the organization's leadership is made up of a bunch of wankers.

"Process cannot replace leadership; but good leadership will ensure that there is a structure in the organization so that every individual will feel fulfilled and contributing."

—JULES MEUNIER

CHAPTER 6:

If you are a butcher,
everything is a piece of meat

I AM PRETTY SURE THE title of this chapter is a politically incorrect statement, particularly since it has nothing to do with food, but hopefully it will illustrate the point. My theory is simply this: while some people are able to adjust and evolve their skills to optimize the benefits of disruptive technologies, systems and processes, others are not. They know what they know and nothing else, and even when they are given new tools to work with, they simply use them in the same way they did the old ones.

I love food and cooking and I admire a fine butcher and his (or her) eye for high-grade meats. The chapter has less to deal with butchers than the attitude if you treat everything the same way, you will lose the subtle or explicit advantages of whatever it is you are working with. As skilled as butchers are, meat is all that they know well and in most cases, meat is all they will ever know well. I don't know about you, but I am quite fine with my butcher sticking to his core competence for the long term. There is nothing wrong in people playing to their strengths as long as both the individual and the manager are of the same belief as to what that is. Personally, for the teams I have always led, flexibility and skill-set evolution are keys to our overall success.

The problem is that not all people are able or willing to keep pace with the rapid and ongoing change of the modern world. In this chapter, I want to talk about the perils of leaders and professionals at all levels who are not capable of transforming the way they operate new tools and technology.

In the high technology field, every few years there is some technological advancement that is heralded as the new solution to ensure competitiveness (be it new services or reduced costs), and being human, we always like to believe in the easy miraculous solutions. Quick and easy solutions to change the fortunes of a company are something like the miracle pills that allow you to eat anything you want while you lose weight, and which, not surprisingly, are a multi-billion dollar business; do not be fooled that they exist

The challenge will always be determining the plan for legacy products and services as the new "cure" is adopted. I have a few examples in mind here, such as The Six Sigma Process, or emerging products such as "Cloud" services. Another relevant example here is the Apple iPad, initially marketed for downloading books as a competitor to the Amazon Kindle, which seemed like a waste of a novel tool. The Apple user community evolved the iPad into a mobile extension of an entertainment and email platform, and coined the term "companion" device.

Where the "cures" are meant to be transformational in nature, it is interesting to observe how experts emerge out of the wood-work to help out with miraculous corporate cures. The same applies to how one can streamline efficient operation through usages of the iPad or similar tablet technologies. You know what they say about the professional students; they never leave the campus. Well there is a similar breed of professional experts on hot topics. They seem to be around for all the new ones. Their business cards may change every year or two, but in the end it seems to always be the same people with different titles. You start wondering if it is the same people doing all the new hot stuff One would ask themselves what about the miracle cure they were "supporting" two years ago? So, whenever you are doing something new that is meant to provide better cost of ownership – and the emphasis here is on better cost of ownership – it is critical to ensure a holistic view is adopted. Trends and "cool" things have a limited shelf life. So when looking at the total cost of ownership – not just getting the systems and processes out of the door, but adding to them and maintaining them – think of the big picture and multi-year view.

A few years ago, IP (Internet Protocol) transformation was the main topic of the day for networks operators. No doubt in my mind, companies like Cisco, Juniper, Alcatel-Lucent made a lot of money selling IP networking gear. Service providers and web based operators were rushing to transform their networks to leverage IP networking equipment. Once they were painfully done, they realized that total cost of ownership of IP networks was actually more expensive than legacy networks. True, the price of the IP equipment was cheaper but so was the offered price of their services. Customers and competition drove down the prices of the services, so in essence without operationalizing the IP equipment with next generation tools and services, the benefits were marginal at best for the expensive undertaking. What happened?

Were all the experts wrong? Maybe, however I am pretty sure there were issues with implementation. By implementation, I do not just mean the development of the technology, but also its operationalization and maintenance. That experience led me to conclude that many organizations don't revisit the cost of ownership in a manner that takes into account the cost of operationalizing the technology and its ongoing maintenance.

I am sure people will say this is a blanket generalization that is not true all the time. It is important to provide not just new technology guidelines, but also operational guidelines (misapplication is a bigger travesty than non-application). Otherwise, once the technology is developed and implemented, the people who operate it will be the same people who operated the old technology, and as good as they are, they will treat both equally drawing on their experience. This results in losing the possibility to operate new technology within the new paradigm. I have loads of examples on this, and none of them fall into the category of failure due to laziness; rather they fall either in the category of not knowing better, or the category of not being able to recognize the need for change on the processes and operations front, which at the end of the day is just as bad as incompetence.

Simply put, new technologies and processes require new paradigms to operationalize them. In the early 2000s, Voice over Internet Protocol (VOIP) was touted as the logical evolution of TDM (time division multiplexing – or circuit switching as most commonly known). True, the new technology is the natural evolution, but the VOIP technology comes with new paradigms to support, operate and maintain. The example here has profound transformational impact. For 30-plus years the world of telephony and networking was based on TDM technologies. With the arrival of VOIP, you would be amazed how many organizations used IP to make things look like TDM. So, companies that treated IP applications like they would legacy network based applications burdened operations and systems needlessly and lost any efficiency they may have obtained through cheaper equipment costs. True, the equipment cost of VOIP was cheaper, but that is only part of the total cost of ownership (TCO). Existing operators have already incurred the cost of deploying TDM. Telephony services were a sunk cost, and replacing the old for the new to get the same functionality is a waste of money, so a holistic view of the TCO is critical.

As a side note, IP equipment, especially Ethernet based interfaces, were an order of magnitude cheaper than their legacy substitutes, yet the overall costs of implementation did not drop. By the way, equipment costs typically represent around 30 per cent of the total cost of ownership on a networking project. This is an area in which numerous networking service providers and networking equipment vendors wasted billions of dollars, and is perhaps worthy of a full chapter.

The main shift between VOIP and TDM is simple. In the TDM world, the telephony service also required the end-to-end network to operate effectively. In the VOIP world, the telephony service was an application that operated on a generic IP transport network which is used by other services and applications such as Internet access and content distribution, television, for example. TELUS embarked on its IP transformation in 2000, and it quickly became clear that to take advantage of the changing technology paradigms, we needed to upgrade the systems and processes. An appropriate program was kicked off soon after to ensure that the true benefits of next generation technologies were realized.

USING C++ TO WRITE FORTRAN — A REAL EXAMPLE

The year was 1990, and there were three technology disruptions in the software development industry:

1   Computer workstations were taking a foot hold as a development environment in place of the computer mainframes. Looking at the business and process impacts, people were used to sharing the computing resource when they developed and worked. Developers were all linked to a central computing platform, and now were offered a stand-alone connected, rather than a shared platform; a very different available computing resource paradigm. So without practicing the new paradigm, they would develop assuming they had centralized computing, which was a waste of the newly introduced platforms which would have enabled them to develop at their own pace independent of the centralized contentious computing platform. Imagine a factory where everyone shared the same tools to get things done. They would be organized differently than a factory where every worker had their own tools.

2   The decentralization of computing gave emergence to programming languages that were designed for software programming re-use. Basically, rather than building each function end to end;

build on other people's work. The whole paradigm of designing building blocks that anyone can use is terribly attractive. Thus, the main benefit that the rise of c and c++ subsequently as an object oriented programming language provided was efficiency and re-use (never forget that technological evolution should always have business benefits). So when c++ (Object oriented code) was launched, people forgot to ensure the benefits and promise were tracked. Object oriented code was intended for people to document their programs and make them available for re-use, resulting in efficiencies on two levels – program re-use and time to market – basically moving software programming from an individual effort to a team effort. So unless, people were properly trained and rewarded for these two outcomes, one would do what one does best. I cannot fault the workers, but rather the leadership for not providing the right guidance.

3   Computer Aided Design (CAD) tools for software development were available to improve programming time and quality. An example is a tool developed by Object Time (I am sure the company has been resold and renamed numerous times since 1992) to help document and automatically generate code with the objective of making software developers more efficient with improved time to market; basically a software management tool that was purposefully built. Up until then, companies typically established their own processes or had in house built tools. The tools would take a high level design and generate software code and documentation for the purpose of collaboration and sharing. Note, prior to this, software developers did not have such holistic software development tools.

The three points above are all good and intuitively beneficial. What happened? Development time doubled, software bugs tripled and over-all costs quadrupled. The developers were used to writing their software and compiling at the end of the day (mainframe training) so no benefits to local computing were realized. In some instances, people would keep working until the end of the day, then compile their software, rather than compile whenever they finished a stand-alone piece of code.

The makeup of a software design team in early 1990's consisted of professionals that had just learned C, having gone through FOR-TRAN, COBOL and BASIC as the main academic programming lan-guages they learned. The corporation gave them C++ training drawing on the knowledge of C. The result was that they ended up using C++ to write FORTRAN. My uncle calls it cloning, which truly fits the bill here. Done right, it provides scalability and re-use; done wrong, it provides a replica of the old. True C++ software was only seen when a sufficient number of younger next-generation engineers, who were taught object oriented programming as a base, started seeding the organization did the programming mess become apparent. The size of the software pro-duced was simply too large and not terribly optimal. Suffice to say that sharp knives are dangerous in the wrong hands, and so the point is simply that when you give people state of the art tools, be sure to pro-vide them with the proper training to optimize their use.

The software tools that were meant to support proper object ori-ented code and document the design were misused. The developers never used tools to write software for them. The traditional reuse tech-niques of "cut & paste" or invoking a software sub-routine call is not a tool. You would not believe the size of code that came out and the amount of needless steps that were incorporated. One of the amusing (actually tear wrenching moments) was when the tool generated 17 possible outcomes for what should have been a TRUE or FALSE out-come. "Crap in; crap out," as the saying goes.

What I am trying to capture here are the direct impacts of leveraging new technology and new tools, in which all too often people end up just using them the way they know best. In the above mentioned case, the impacts were disastrous. I shared one of my personal examples with C++. Another is GM building the Saturn business unit only to compete with themselves and not the traditional Japanese car manufacturers.

$24.99 ALL YOU CAN USE — NORTH AMERICA WIDE

The introduction of Voice Over Internet Protocol (VOIP), or packet telephony, in North America first seemed like the great price saviour for consumers. Even though things are cheaper these days, long distance revenues used to subsidize local telephony and local telephony was made available universally to urban and rural areas, which I would say was holistically better for the overall citizen. This is true for countries like Canada and the USA with a large rural population. I do not intend to pontificate and lament the good old days of government blessed monopoly. But our current reality is that most rural areas in North America are at their lowest point in terms of telecommunications capabilities, as the battle ground for higher earnings is in urban North America, which is where almost of the telecommunications connectivity and services investments are focused.

Have you ever thought why the cable and internet telephony operators launched a flat rate telephony service? The answer is not to make the world a better place and to help the consumer. I doubt the answer is that they wanted to offer a price competitive service compared to the telephone companies. They would have rather launched a higher margin service, complete with pay for usage and area code price sensitivity.

The answer is simple. It is very difficult to monitor a phone call by the destination and per-minute when the service is based on IP addresses and packets. IP addresses are owned by companies and have no geographical connotations. The cost to build a billing and metering system to differentiate prices on area codes, time of day and duration of call would have been prohibitive; they would have had to replicate what the traditional telephone companies invested millions of dollars and many years of evolution and sophistication in. Was this good or bad? Not sure, however, the cable companies are succeeding in re-pricing the telephony market in North America. We could say they stumbled on this by mistake, saying new technology needs a new business model, and for cable operators, telephony is a new technology. Regardless, I am pretty sure that to replicate the traditional telephony model would have been a major barrier to entry owing to systems costs and delays. Another telephony vendor, VONAGE, applies the same business model for the same reasons.

On a side note, the Internet is getting overloaded and something eventually will have to give. Be ready to pay for usage and differentiated internet services sometime soon. Internet access is a utility, and eventually, like all utilities, there will be metering in place. I could write books about the Internet and its usage patterns, but I simply want to point out that unmetered usage is never the end state. Water, which covers most of the earth's surface, is metered and monetized. Numerous futuristic science fiction books and movies have dealt that subject up, and one of my all-time favourites is *Dune* by Frank Herbert (published in 1965). Metering the Internet, which is a man-made resource, is only a matter of time. But again I digress.

SUMMARY

I admit that I may be overly critical here regarding the issue of operationalizing new technologies. It is a waste of corporate time and resources to do the old stuff in new ways when the intention was to transform the business with new benefits and services. The good news is I have started seeing complementary practices or trends emerging to address this issue. They are geared around proper buy-in and adoption of new technologies and processes from all stakeholders – basically explaining the rationale and developing metrics for the new systems to everyone touched by them. The days of top-down design are over when it comes to introducing transformation technologies and processes. Note the leadership and decision making still needs to be done. The key is to approach new services with a new business and operational model and to ensure everyone operates in the new world in an appropriate way. Buy-in and education are required to ensure that the people operating the new tools and the people designing them marry design and architecture with application and operations.

Incidentally, some new management techniques such as fair thought process and governance have emerged to help secure corporate stakeholder "buy-in." Both fair thought processes and governance address the buy-in of all the stakeholders for new tools, practices and processes. They are getting a lot of coverage in the executive management training courses, which is a good thing. After all, proper buy-in and stakeholder consultation are good first steps, and far more effective in the long run than simple coercion. Both of these formalize the age-old approach of playing as a team and sharing the game plan and results with everyone.

Above all, when introducing new processes and technologies, ensure that the people who are to receive and use them understand what needs to be done to properly leverage these new tools. I truly believe practical end-to-end processes captured by individuals who are intimate with the new products and services are the only way to ensure the benefits are realized. And sadly when "meat" is no longer the popular staple, I doubt that all of the butchers can be retrained, so some must be invited to leave.

So if you are told to shut up and do something in a certain way because that is how it has been done before or that this is the wonderful new world without the proper explanation, the person telling you is a wanker.

If you are told to invest time and effort on activities that will yield trivial results, the person telling you is a wanker.

And if you are told one size fits all, you are listening to yet another wanker.

> *"Never neglect details. When everyone's mind is dulled or distracted, the leader must be doubly vigilant."*
> — COLIN POWELL

CHAPTER 7:

Commoditizing Leadership

Jack Welch

"If you pick the right people and give them the opportunity to spread their wings and put compensation as a carrier behind it, you almost don't have to manage them."

— JACK WELCH

GREAT QUOTE from a great man, but why haven't his ideas automatically translated into success for so many other organizations? Whether his intention was to make more money or simply help corporate America, Jack Welch has commoditized leadership. Sometimes I wonder if his genius has been an evil for corporate America. What I mean by commoditized leadership is writing best-selling leadership books with "easy" to follow processes for success, all of them subtracting his personal leadership out of the success equation. His track record sold the story and numerous corporations implemented his strategies of supply chain and "spans and layers" on the human resource front, but very few were met with similar success. I have no proof of this fact as I doubt anyone would admit failure, however, the reverse is true – no one has been touting their great transformational success due to implementing spans and layers.

Two things are at play here – commoditizing leadership and providing artificial hope for sinking companies. Not every corporation has a Jack Welch at the helm and, more importantly, what helped General Electric may not work for everyone. Corporations thought Welch's "Spans and Layers" theory, which is merely a vehicle to ensure clear horizontal and vertical communication of roles and responsibilities, would by itself fix their ailing fortunes.

I need to be explicit here. I truly believe that Jack Welch wrote his first book to leave a legacy that others might use and implement his principles. What is shameful is the simplification of the execution and the discounting of Jack Welch's personal leadership that was key to GE's success. Also shameful are the numerous sequels, the motivation for which was probably more financial than that of leaving a legacy. Some may say I disrespect Jack Welch, which is not true, but I believe his commoditization of leadership, and more importantly, his success in doing so among naïve corporate leaders is something I do resent. The blind implementation of processes without the knowledge of why and how to apply them is a waste of corporate effort that delivers no real value.

COMMODITIZATION OF LEADERSHIP

There is a huge problem with "transformational formulas" as described by proven leaders like Jack Welch. They capture the process or method to success without describing the leadership and passion that energized the organization, which to me is more important than the process itself. These "formulas" do not take into account their personal contribution, commitment and the specific rationale of why and how. If leadership was a magical formula, people who get to be CEO would be terribly savvy and we would never have companies go bust or run into the ground. The truth is that what worked in a certain circumstance for a certain leader may not work for those in other situations. Giving an example here is useless, as we could write many books citing companies such as General Motors, Nortel Networks, Enron and others, whose leaders failed in spite of the teachings of Jack Welch and others. Personally I am a book worm. Learning from other people's experiences is important, but one should always apply the whole reasoning and not just implement the process.

SPANS AND LAYERS

We cannot have a chapter that talks about Jack Welch and not talk about his "Spans and Layers" organizational structure recommendations. In Jack's ideal world, the number of layers of management between the CEO and the general employee population is seven, and the span of control of each manager, irrespective of layer, is six to 14 direct reports.

Sounds good on paper, and it worked for Jack and GE, but I have to say that implementing Spans and Layers without measurable targets is like changing one's undergarments. Not sure about you, but my suspicion is that no one knows or cares about your underwear, but you. If what you are doing internally has no apparent value to the outside world, or if there is no mechanism in place to measure the overall effectiveness of the changes, then you have engaged in a purely academic exercise. Outside of GE, there have been few successful implementations of spans and layers; no corporations have come forward stating that spans and layers saved their ailing fortunes. We should always remember Jack implemented spans and layers to ensure communication and control. I do believe ensuring a manageable span of control and layers in the organization is important, but each function and each corporation differs. What worked for Manufacturing may not be ideal for Research and Development. Cisco Systems, one of the more successful telecommunications equipment manufacturers, has over 10 layers in some areas between the CEO, John Chambers, and the employees (Jack advocated that seven was ideal). I doubt we could say anything about Cisco other than acknowledge their success and proven ability to weather economic downturns. Even what seemed like an isolated extravagant move – purchasing Scientific Atlanta – has turned into one of Cisco's next-generation thrusts for content delivery. Cisco has maintained its global leadership in the networking space and emerged as the premier leader in video networking by understanding and providing a complete suite of products as seen by their "video-scape" launch in 2011.

Spans and Layers are not a solution to fix a corporation's declining fortunes or something to do to feel good about themselves in the name of employee satisfaction and competitiveness. My own feeling is that when you are knee deep in quick sand, your top concern cannot be if your hair is well groomed. The travesty is, however, that organizations often respond to crises by implementing new systems and procedures that deliver no value to their clients. What is it that the spans and layers remedy is meant to fix? There can be many solutions to any given problem, and textbooks rarely provide solutions. Keep in mind that when you are forcing a fatigued organization to make changes that do not improve customer, employee or shareholder value, you are creating an even more troubled one. Thanks Jack! At the same time though, do we blame Jack Welch or do we blame the various leaders that took the quick fix? Both are to blame. And the victims are the corporation and employees, not to mention the Human Resource department, which is rendered impotent.

SUMMARY

I do not want to take away from the genius of Jack Welch. He recognized that he had a massive communications and supply chain issue, thus his Spans and Layers structure, guided by his personal leadership was the right thing to do. An argument can be made that General

Electric has weathered the latest global economic downturn because of what he put in place years ago. I am not sure Spans and Layers is an issue facing Google or Facebook today. I truly believe Spans and Layers is something that is proven in highly operational environments such as manufacturing, construction, the military. And I also believe it is, at best, corporate overhead for teams engaged in innovation, research or sales. Who knows, maybe in five years Google's fortune will start declining and one way for them to "differentiate" may perhaps be Spans and Layers, although I doubt Google customers will care about the company's internal structure.

So if you are asked to implement a process that will cause you grief with no explicit explanation on the overall benefits, the new process is a wanker

If you are told there is a magical solution to real problems that have been festering for years, leave it as a sequel for *Jack and the Bean Stalk*, rather than submitting to the preposterous theory of a wanker.

And if you are told cosmetic surgery will make you a smarter person, you are either talking to a cosmetic surgeon, or a bona fide wanker.

CHAPTER 8:

Human Resources: Friend or Foe?

Human resource (HR) departments are a critical part of every large organization. They are an essential support element, for as we all go about doing what we do best, we need someone to oversee compensation, benefits and employee relations. This chapter captures some of my experiences and insights working with HR.

ACADEMIC HR ORGANIZATIONS

I have to start this section with my history with HR. I started my working career in 1987 in Research and Development. Like all good technologists in a research and development organization, I believed anything but technology was corporate overhead. Frankly, my perception of HR was simply an organization that focused on re-inventing performance and benefit measurement procedures, always with good intentions to retain talent at the lowest cost or effort. It seemed that every couple of years, there were new forms and new processes, yet the pay and performance usually stayed the same, if not less. Note this is not true if one was a superstar, but then the rules never quite apply there.

Suffice it to say, my early experiences left me unimpressed. Actually, I recall one incident when HR supported blocking my move to another team for almost a year. As I mentioned earlier, harmful rotation is when the organization arbitrarily moves you around without any consideration to your personal aspirations and core strengths. I was in an area that was not terribly rewarding, both career wise and on a personal level. I had to get an offer from a competitor, Ericsson, at that time to force the move. So I felt that the interaction with HR was less than desirable, to say the least.

Then I became a manager, and HR was suddenly a reality to deal with for practical necessities such as performance analysis, headcount management, talent acquisition and the like. I would like to be clear; HR folks are decent, hard-working and well-meaning people, but without the proper leadership in their executive ranks, they often become nothing more than tactical administrators. Administration is a critical part of their jobs, but they have a larger role of being the trusted partner for the employee. A little background here might shed some light on what I am talking about.

NO COLLAR MANAGEMENT ERA

Like most young employees in the 1980s, the myth that an MBA would open doors was very alluring. So I embarked on an MBA part time at the University of Ottawa, which I never finished. The course work was a breeze, however, the course times were lousy, as were the professors' office hours, so I decided to abandon that pursuit. Tough to do a degree when you are also trying to focus on your career.

Parts of the overall obligatory course work were two organizational behaviour courses. I am sure things have changed, but at that time most of the cases were about how to make employees happy and engaged – a good idea. The course was definitely geared towards the legacy notion of workers and managers. In the legacy HR world, we, the university educated employees, were primed to be the managers, as it seemed that education and higher degrees represented a demarcation point. I recall the case studies, which were centered on getting factory workers more natural light or to beautify their environment by adding a few plants, none of which applies to an engineering environment where one manages their peers in the so-called "no-collar workplace." Although some of the conventional human resource management courses are now out of date, I see universities and consulting institutions modernizing to address industry's more current needs. Overall, things are much better now. For example, our HR organization at TELUS is confronting the so-called Generation Y issues, and specifically how to ensure the organization is providing a challenging work place for them, something that all good corporations should be addressing today.

My intention is not to discuss Gen Y here, however, we should not ignore how new entrants to the work force are increasingly demanding an environment that they would like rather than an environment they could supposedly adapt to. In addition, they do not believe in the classical pay-your-dues at every level, but rather believe if they have the talent they should be recognized for it. On that point, I am torn between unleashing the talent, or putting it on a slow broil and seasoning it. I am sure a happy medium will emerge, or the Gen Y talent will leave, as their loyalty will always be tied to their job satisfaction.

In any case, it is important for organizations to never overlook the value of young "untrained" recruits who come with a clean slate to make things happen. They can be your best asset. At the same time though, good organizations must be on the lookout for those that appear to be among the most promising and talented, but who are in fact merely wankers in training. I am a Montreal Canadiens fan, and there is no question their success (maybe not in the past few years) has always been their farm team. They never embraced the higher payroll paradigm, but always had a great farm team. They also had a great brand in the hockey world and the prestige of playing for the Montreal Canadiens ensured they got good talent, but I can recall many instances in which the Canadiens management team demonstrated that talent alone would not suffice.

I remember, for example, when they released Patrick Roy, considered one of the best hockey goalies ever, on the belief that he was simply not a team player. They clearly valued the team more than a single individual and his talent in this case. Today they are considered one of the more talented younger teams in the National hockey League, and one that isn't afraid to weed out wankers regardless of the level of their talent.

Admittedly, we take a lot of things about the workplace environment for granted, but the evolution of HR education has not kept up to industry's needs. So, it is not surprising to see how ill equipped HR teams have been to deal with technology and research and development environments. So exactly how do they become a trusted partner for the employees, the managers and corporation? Let's not forget HR departments exist to make things more optimal for their organizations. Nothing wrong there, that is what the shareholders pay them to do. The relationship with HR is a two way street, I learned early in life that even though it may seem more difficult to work with them than to ignore them, the rewards are definitely worth it.

CATHERINE MOSER-MAXWELL

The year was 2000 and I still felt HR was corporate overhead, re-enforcing in my mind that HR was an organization of "form" pushers. Needless to say my perception did not help me appreciate the role of HR beyond paperwork.

A turning point in my relationship with HR was when I interviewed Catherine Moser-Maxwell. Being invited to interview my HR prime (now the word "HR partner" is in vogue) was something novel to me. I felt I had nothing to lose. Let me frame the actual environment at the time. I was Vice President of Wireless Network Engineering at Nortel Networks, managing a large global engineering team with the looming economic downturn of 2000.

There were four internal candidates for the role of HR prime for the wireless engineering team. Not being an expert, they all seemed like good people and seasoned HR professionals. When I asked the question of what the role would mean to them, I had varying answers from "challenging opportunity" to "I enjoy working with technical teams." Nothing stuck except Catherine's answer. I will never forget what she told me. "I want to make you more successful in managing your people." A simple statement, but to me, it moved her from the HR overseer to the HR partner role. And for the first time in my work life, HR became a critical part of my organization. I tell you, there may not be a lot of Catherines out there, but I would recommend you spend time with your HR partner before you rule them out. She showed me what good HR people can do, and that raised my expectations. At the same time, once these expectations were identified, I can say I have been blessed with many good HR partners. Now I know what to look for in an HR partner.

EMOTIONAL INTELLIGENCE AND APPLIED INTELLIGENCE

I knew there had to be something to help me out in my job as a people manager. I got promoted to manager in 1994 and I needed to be more successful managing my team. I embarked on a literature scan and read loads on leadership and teamwork (to no avail according to some of my team members). There is no shortage of management literature, but my quest was not to eat the whole ox, just to learn how to always pick the right people and retain them. Or more importantly, the right people to work with me as a leader. I know it sounds like motherhood, but the teams I worked in and with have been instrumental in both my successes and failures. It's true that you are only as good as the people around you.

In the good old days, before my numerous knee and back surgeries (I was an ardent soccer player), it was clear the winning team was not necessarily the team with all the super stars. Rather, it was the team with the right composition in which everyone played position and supported their colleagues when needed. I could also write a few pages on why absolute rigor in playing position is not advantageous, beginning with how it propagates the "my part of the ship is not sinking" mentality. I am sure there are a lot of critics about playing position at any cost. In any case, I believe that the key is to execute on one's roles and responsibilities, but also to help out proactively if the team needs it.

In team efforts, you need enough super stars to anchor the effort, but more importantly, you need a balanced, cohesive and unselfish machine. Discovering this helped me to understand that my best team-mates were not necessarily the ones that had the highest grades at university.

Football (soccer to North Americans) fans will no doubt recall the efforts of Real Madrid (The Galactic Team) in the early 2000's. They had players who were considered among the best in their position, and with the highest payroll in the world. However, the team's track record did not positively reflect the dollar spent on their payroll. True, their merchandising arm was making huge profits, but their football track record left a lot to be desired. I am not exactly sure why they did not perform to expectations. No doubt they were a team to be feared, but somehow the various talented players did not transform into the team everyone expected. Perhaps too many super stars and not enough team play. At the end of the day, the whole did not exceed the sum of the parts, which is a desired outcome in terms of synergies. The key is to get the most out of the individual talents in the context of the overall team success.

So how does one pick the right balance between talent, synergy and heart? Some time ago, I came across Daniel Goldman's work on "emotional intelligence." Goldman pioneered the work around the emotional quotient (EQ). As the world was busy with IQ, he talked about the value to EQ. I tell you, the field of emotional or "applied" intelligence was a revelation for me. It explained a lot. For example, it explained why the smartest people are not necessarily the best team players, leaders or contributors. The EQ concept that success is a combination of raw intelligence, and more importantly, how well it is applied (attitude and personality) was a great explanation. Once I started digging into it, I saw multiple forms of it. A lot of the sophisticated sales assessments look for emotional intelligence. Interestingly, the sales industry where it is "sink and die" or "kill", has had assessment tests for applied intelligence for many years, the same for the insurance industry.

I recall my interactions with Steve Baillargeon, a talented engineer, and I would say one of the best that I had the pleasure to work with. Steve, as an engineering student, played for the McGill University football team and had an option of being drafted to the Canadian Football League, but he opted for a career in engineering, and for that I am grateful. I probed into Steve's academic background and found out he was a solid performer, but not one of the top in his class. His skill set was being able to translate complex systems into easily digestible operational steps – a true architect as captured earlier. My basic feeling is that high grades are an indicator of IQ and the ability to harness and understand tools whose application is not proven until later on. Translating IQ into EQ is the desired outcome for any successful individual. Going back to the Real Madrid example – you probably guessed I like to cheer for them as a football team – they failed to truly translate their raw individual talent (IQ) into a well synchronized winning team (EQ).

If you search for the folks that are your anchor points, you will realize that you need people who have a very high EQ. I would bet most of these individuals were not the ones with a 90-plus per cent average at university. I cannot claim that after my research I became a better leader or manager, but I was definitely more aware of the importance of having sufficient reserves of EQ within leadership teams. You realize superstars are very bright people with scarce skills that are critical to the projects. Applied intelligence and skill sets are important characteristics, and not simply raw gifts. I can think of another football example that might help shed further light on this high-level concept. The 2004 European Football Championships were held in Portugal, and the Greek national team were the surprise winners. One of the biggest long shots in the history of the sport, they did not do it because of their superstars, as they had no players listed in the top 25 footballers of Europe. They beat the football power houses and the local favourite Portuguese team because they were a cohesive, unselfish team and had a strategy.

From a football (soccer) point of view, their strategy and game was boring. For the football enthusiasts, they played like the Italian National Team without the flare and the ego. The whole team was on defence and opportunistically attacked, however, that was all they needed to do, and by playing it smart, they won the championship. This is a case where the whole was much greater than the sum of its parts. The great power houses of football such as Italy and Germany went home in defeat. Come to think of it, Real Madrid could have learned a lot from the Greeks that year.

I hope the mixing and matching of analogies between football teams and HR support did not confuse you. Team success is about good leadership and HR's role is not to do the leader's job for them, but to support them in their people management endeavours.

SOCIALISM AND ENTITLEMENT

Let's be clear, the top objective for HR is to ensure the organization has the right skill sets performing at an optimal level. But as their titles suggest, the raw material they work with is humanity, and humanity has its frailties. There are mechanisms for compassion and leniency, but the truth remains that if the company can be compassionate and lenient at the lowest possible cost, they will. If I am a shareholder of the company, I love them for it.

There is a belief that one can always cut back by 10 per cent, be it people or spending. I subscribe that there are always efficiencies that can be leveraged, however, academic statements and actions rarely work more than once or twice. An organization cannot shed 10 per cent every quarter, or cut employee benefits every quarter, or downgrade their tools and services every quarter. A clear and explicit direction of abandoning businesses and a holistic plan are required. On headcount reductions, one guide I advise my team to use is rather than pick who to fire, pick who to keep. This makes the prioritization effort easier and more objective. If you had to keep one person in your organization, you can easily start prioritizing, then the next and so forth to produce a de-facto ranking system. We all know how to do this exercise. Remember when we were kids picking team mates for dodge ball? Who said growing up was easy?

Nothing is more difficult than telling someone who is average that they are an average performer. You know what they say, if you buy people at their market value and sell them at what they think they are worth, one would be a millionaire. Why? Since the day we were born, our parents told us we were special and could do anything once we put our minds to it until reality – the workplace – got in the way. We then realize what it means to be human and part of the workplace eco-system. I believe if the organization reached out to its employees with the choices of either headcount reductions or voluntary pay reductions across the board, they would be surprised to find that pay reductions would be the preferred pill.

My recommendation is to start pay reductions with the executives (and I am one of those). I believe companies like Motorola had such programs. Something they never advertised for fear of heralding they were in trouble, I actually think they demonstrated true leadership, but what do I know? I am a technologist, not a financial analyst. I understand that the market would view that as a signal of desperation, but I disagree. We all tighten our belts in our personal lives, defer renovations and reduce our "discretionary expenses" such as entertainment.

Maybe a good measure would be a 10 per cent pay reduction across the board, but that would look bad. HR departments have to play their role so no one can blame them. I advocate looking at efficiencies where ever they may be. My only concern is let's not try to build corporate programs that substitute honest speak. People are smart and they do not need fake programs that fake their value. If they accept the programs it is not because they are "sold" on them

At the end of the day, what "average" people need when working in tough economic environments and in companies facing cost pressure is for leaders to find a clear, but reasonably compassionate way of saying something to the effect of: "Buddy, you are a great asset where you are. Your pay for performance is what we believe is your market value. Thanks for everything and keep up the good work." People deemed average by the organization are not stupid, therefore honesty is critical in managing them effectively.

I believe the acceptance of all new performance strategies would be a simpler task if corporations were honest about people's net worth. We all have experienced examples when the pot was sweetened for someone who was deemed critical outside the corporate guideline. I recall a couple of years ago at a management retreat when an HR executive tried to explain to a bunch of engineers why a new compensation package was better for them. When you have a number of engineers that enjoy mathematics and are capable of writing modelling software, you better know your facts. Clearly the new performance package was simply moving the average down and increasing the discrimination on who is truly a good performer. Since most people are average, this did not come as a terribly welcome move. I would like to add that there is nothing wrong in being average. God have mercy if the world was made of 50 per cent superstars and 50 per cent under achievers. Being somewhere in the middle is normal. The key is to ensure that performance and reward expectations are fair and well-articulated. Where would we be without our team – our whole team?

To be fair to HR organizations, the management ranks also have to display leadership and provide feedback. There is nothing wrong in being a nine-to-five employee that executes on what is being asked of them. I guess managers are like parents sometime and sugar coat the reality of the work and reward. I have yet to see parents who do not think their child is the next Einstein or Bill Gates or more likely Sidney Crosby. A positive attitude is great, but if the raw talent and its successful application are not realized, then the result is average performance, hopefully solid average performance.

SUMMARY

It took a while, but I have a lot of respect for good HR teams. Good HR people provide fantastic tools if leveraged by an individual or leader the right way. Their objective is not to make you happy, but to ensure a good balance between driving optimal performance for the organization and keeping valuable resources satisfied. The key word is valuable. My advice is simple. We all believe that we are valuable resources. The question is exactly how valuable are we, and that is where the disconnect happens. Your options are simple: change jobs, remain frustrated or be content that your employer is fair.

So if you believe you are being shafted, leave or risk becoming a wanker.

If you have a new program that makes you feel good but does not increase your reward and recognition, the program is a wanker.

If you are told you are fantastic and you are loved, yet others seem to make more money and get rewarded, look inside first and ask yourself, am I really as good as I think I am, or am I a dreamer and a wanker?

*"Often we enjoy the comfort of opinion
without the discomfort of thought."*
— JOHN F. KENNEDY

CHAPTER 9

It's not you, but maybe your sources

I BRIEFLY MENTIONED the tremulous year I had after the Nortel acquisition of Bay Networks. After we realized that service providers and carrier grade enterprises needed different focus than basic enterprises (reliability being the key), we re-aligned the organization into two business units: service provider and enterprise. The logical step was moving my core engineering team from predominantly enterprise data sales into service provider data sales support, a good interim step and one that provided much relief by keeping two masters happy: the corporation (my boss) and our clients. At that time, the data/packet service provider business was dwarfed by the rapidly growing optical and wireless product lines. The reality is the corporation's attention was on $30 billion of optical and wireless product revenues rather than a mere $1 billion in revenues of data products.

To put this into context, the year was 1998 and IP was considered a "hot" technology by many, but Nortel's top line revenue growth was from fibre optical and wireless infrastructure sales.

Even after streamlining sales along enterprise and service provider lines, Nortel recognized that we needed the product development focus on these different market segments. We were simply not keeping up with the competition in the service provider and service provider grade enterprise space. They appointed Jules Meunier as head for data research and development (including product line management) and he quickly realized the importance of a clear delineation between the two segments at that time. He split enterprise and service provider and took over as general manager of the data service provider business unit. Meanwhile, the enterprise development product team and support organization all remained in the Enterprise Data Networks (EDN) business unit, and in spite of all its great talent, Nortel fared disastrously in that space.

It is noteworthy to mention that Jules Meunier was previously head of sales and marketing for Nortel's GSM wireless business unit. He brought with him a wealth of technology leadership expertise working across multiple cultures (Europe and North America), but did not have the actual IP/data technology experience. As I explained earlier, Jules emerged as a great leader for the division and was able to leverage his strengths into moving our division into the global leadership position in our space – a great example of where rotation done right was a brilliant move.

Three weeks after Jules assumed leadership of the service provider data business unit, I was getting terribly frustrated at not being able to share with him what I thought about the business. Jules at that time was having intensive meetings with his team and our clients to get an understanding of the challenges ahead. So three weeks with me not being involved in the thick of redefining what needs to be done was like a slow death to me (call it ego, concern or the need to be an insider). I became more and more anxious to have a heart-to-heart with him. This was especially true since I felt that moving my team back into the product group (similar to the 1996 organization) was the right thing to do. Suffice it to say, I was not terribly patient then and, come to think of it, I am not terribly patient now either. So after a few weeks, I believe I left Jules a nasty voice message indicating that our team tends to work with most of the service providers globally and if he wanted a practical view of what was happening on the ground, my team and I would be the ones to chat with.

30 MINUTES

His assistant at that time, Carolyn Spence, scheduled for me 30 minutes with him. The 30 minutes resulted in a couple of hours and a wonderful subsequent work and personal relationship. I crammed my two years of frustration over product direction and declining client care into that conversation. I have to say he was in listen mode, although perhaps a bit skeptical about the over-enthused engineer who told him we were in deep trouble. Needless to say, I left feeling much better having aired my concerns, but also wondering if I would be fired.

The chat constituted another turning point in my career. Jules formally requested that my team, which at the time was part of Sales, move over to the Product group. For that, I am ever grateful, because I had the chance to work for one of the best managers in the world.

A few months into the new organization, I learned something about my boss, and that was that he liked to have all his information before making a move. Good, bad, or ugly, it was his style, and he always tried to get more than one or two data points before formulating his view.

Interestingly, after a while I outright told him that he spent too much time before acting, and that I was usually right, especially where it relates to how we make our products work for our customers. I will never forget his response: "Ibrahim, the issue is not you, but maybe your sources." As a manager, he correctly believed that in any situation in which the stakes were high, it was his job to check the reliability of sources, including the people I relied upon for accurate data. The technical term for this thought process is "triangulation." I know process experts would probably shudder when I call it "multiple data points." I believe an invaluable lesson was learned: always get multiple data points (opinions) and triangulate. On a more subtle note, this also applies when we think we are so smart and know what to do and react immediately. This is especially true when we mobilize efforts into action based on one data point.

I am reminded of how often organizations overreact when something goes wrong. You see that all the time, when a major project goes astray, and a bunch of highly priced resources (I call this executive pollution) launch themselves to fix the same problem in different ways. It would have been easier if they changed the project leader and then gave that one individual the authority to conduct a thorough investigation (acquiring multiple data points) to decide what was needed, and then begin to fix the problem. Instead, what we more commonly see is a number of people launching themselves into fixing a problem armed with information obtained from a single data point, rather than having the luxury or benefit of knowing the bigger picture.

The reality is that a few months into the project with multiple "bright" thinkers, the project sometimes winds up being fixed in competing ways, resulting in major frustration for all and the organization burns lots of unplanned operating expenses. That further erodes the already low margin on the deal, particularly if it was "strategic" to start with.

In a nutshell, people in general do not intentionally lie, but rather, they sometimes base their assessments on just one or two data points. Whether it is to impress others with their responsiveness or whether they have a high academic IQ and have all the answers, the net result is increased frustration and a loss in productivity and profit.

One more thing, it is amazing how much information can be gathered talking to the junior folks on the team. My view is to never penalize these folks, who are trying to help using the information they have, as limited in scope as it may be. They do not have much political power to lose, and they are basing their information on what they know. The key is the appropriate collection of accurate data points.

SUMMARY

Always get all the facts before taking decisive action. I am not advocating endless analysis leading to "analysis paralysis," but I now know better than to base actions on one data point or rash decisions. At the same time though, I remain a firm believer that experience and intelligence enable you to develop a gut feel that you can often count on. Although you definitely do not want to lose the intuitive efforts that often make wonders, double checking never hurts. When the lives of thousands of people and millions of dollars are at stake, get a second opinion, or even a third. It's interesting how we apply triangulation to medical analysis as an acceptable standard, but tend to overlook the same precaution in business.

If you are asked to provide feedback, never miss the opportunity. You never know how that will shape the outcome. If you pass on the opportunity, you are a wanker.

Always triangulate, especially on matters concerning large projects, or you run the risk of being a wanker.

"One small step up the mountain often widens your perspective in all directions."
— EDWARD HOWARD GRIGGS, author and philosopher

CHAPTER 10:

Customer Value Management

AS A RESEARCHER, I never paid attention to customer satisfaction measures. After all I was answering to a higher authority, that of technical excellence and innovation. With the luxury of hindsight, I can now see that was a bullshit attitude.

The first time I paid attention to any customer measure was in 1994 when my bonus had a customer satisfaction component. Weird! I thought that was clearly unfair. After all, I worked my ass off and if the rest of the organization couldn't deliver, then why should I be penalized? My part of the ship wasn't sinking. And I have to say I have been using that phrase ever since to mock people who claim success when the overall project has failed. At junior levels, it is unfair to punish the soldier for failure, however the officers at all levels must be held accountable.

When something impacts your paycheque, you start paying attention to it. In 1994, Nortel had what they called a customer satisfaction (C Sat) program. Customers were asked to rate how happy they were with Nortel and Nortel products. It was on a scale from 0 to 5, and a 4 or 5 indicated customers were happy and had no issues.

A side note here, C Sat impacted the sales organization the most as they had a much larger weighting on C Sat results for their bonus. You have to admire the sales guys, who being intelligent and realizing the impact on their payout due to C Sat, easily manipulated the process and they were getting high customer satisfaction scores resulting in major bonus payouts while we were losing ground to the competition in revenue and market share. The program did not require a genius to produce those results. The sales guys would simply ask only friendly customers to fill in the survey and ply them with food and wine as an added security measure. Nortel got brilliant results, but was losing market share and customers. This was in the context of my division (Data Networks) back in 1995.

TWO HOURS WON'T KILL YOU

My manager at that time, Doug Alteen (an excellent manager and a good friend), asked me to attend a presentation on a brand new C Sat program that was about to be rolled out. As usual, considering myself a technical superstar and highly recognized, I felt it was a waste of my time. In my mind, it was yet another stupid corporate program. What clinched my attendance at the unveiling of the new customer program was Doug promising a decent meal and wine after the event. I was sold on attending, I never pass up an invitation for decent food and wine, and after all Doug was my boss.

I attended apathetically at first, but then realized that something new was being presented. What they shared with us were not C Sat scores, but rather how Nortel was perceived against the competition and the surveying mechanism was by a third party (to minimize the friendly manipulation of the score).

The program was called Customer Value Management (cvm), and it represented a huge turning point in my career with the understanding of how I affected the bottom line. It seemed like a point of divine revelation at the time to discover that life is not a race against oneself, and that there is a world out there. Not only that, but I gained a mechanism that would allow me and my colleagues to increase our value to our client. Not to mention, I also gained a long-time friend, Scott

Hendricks, a pioneer in CVM and globally recognized authority on the subject, as he and his team won several global awards for their CVM program while at Nortel. Believe it or not, Nortel's CVM predicted the growing distance between the organization and its clients, and the fact that CVM scores were dropping should have been a warning heeded by the senior executives. The greater impact to Nortel was that they built their customer strategies on half-truths, as the voice of the customer was not heeded.

I have to say the two hours spent at an Ottawa hotel's meeting room proved to be priceless. In hindsight, my advice today is keep an open mind and be willing to try things at least once.

A METRIC THAT MATTERS

I was excited that for the first time there was a comparison on how well we fared against the competition. CVM had numerous metrics based on business pillars, and I worked with Scott and the team to evaluate if systems and sales engineering was a pillar that resonated with customers. Indeed it was. We measured it and realized we were behind Cisco, our number one competitor, and so we put a plan in place with regular monitoring. I was pleased that over a couple of years we passed the competition in our domain. Still, we were one small piece of the overall equation, but being the best is always good to know – not that my ego or that of my team needed too much help.

The ability to translate our specific role into something of customer value was huge. Our score and how we could keep moving it upwards was something that all levels of the organization could relate to. How novel is it having a metric that is relevant to the customers, the employees and the shareholders? Customers who value your products and services over those of your competitors are terribly loyal, which translates to repeat business and proactive involvement with the strategic direction, and ultimately a true partnership between buyer and seller. This is truly music to the shareholder community, as customers believe their supplier is actually working for them.

One question I like to ask sales people is, "are you selling or is the client buying?" When the customer buys, then the product is another commodity, but when the sales person is selling and partnering, then they are solving a customer's problem.

ABUSED CVM

My sentiment towards CVM was not unique, and it became in vogue to implement CVM in large organizations. There is lots of literature out there to share the process and results of CVM. As usual, consulting firms sprouted out of nowhere to consult on CVM programs, their design and their implementation. We covered consultant DNA earlier and noted how they rarely owned the operationalization of their recommendation, and CVM was no different. Operationalizing CVM was just as important as gathering the data. Customers are not willing to invest time and effort in responding to surveys (valid or not) if they see no value. I rarely fill out surveys that do not indicate what will be done with the results. I would rather do housework than participate in a survey that only makes people feel good about themselves.

The two covenants to make CVM work are relevant data and follow-up. If the data is not relevant, one cannot take action concerning what needs to be done. The CVM exercise would serve nothing but to frustrate the business leaders, and potentially the whole organization. So do it right, or else implement the legacy C Sat type of programs, which are cheaper and will make you feel good about yourself irrespective of reality.

One of the worst things to happen with abused CVM is CVM on steroids. That happens when CVM professionals gather reams of data. Drinking from a fire hose is not a pleasurable experience, nor particularly thirst-quenching. You end up with endless data that looks you in the face with no way for you to take action and a large department that reminded you that you can do better, but without the support to establish action priorities. Unless the data is manageable and actionable, it is tough to operationalize. For myself and my team, three key initiatives seems to be the optimal number that can be absorbed from a purely practical view as it is difficult for an organization to focus on numerous improvement measures. I recall receiving a CVM score sheet of 43 metrics. "Great," I said to myself sarcastically, not having a clue where to start, or which one would have the biggest impact.

Another ugly side of CVM is whitewashing. I recall one year at Nortel, the results were not that attractive. People hate bad news, and the decision was to sweep the results under the carpet so as not to impact the bonus of those who depended on CVM for their pay-out. At that time, Scott and his team stood their ground and, suffice it to say, Scott became a Nortel Alumnus. I am sure the senior executives were humouring only themselves.

I recall my statistics university professor many moons ago. Whenever we came up with an answer and got excited with our interpretation he would tell us that statistics are like a bathing suit: what they show is nice, but what they hide may be ghastly or beautiful.

I guess my professor could have predicted the financial reporting woes of North America 20 years before. Everything was rosy for Enron and MCI and Nortel until the financial data was re-interpreted. I am not an expert on financial reporting, but I am not sure Sarbanes-Oxley has fixed things. I truly believe that the interpretation of numbers is never an exact science.

Another abused form of CVM is not enough actionable data. I recall that when TELUS introduced IPTV in 2006, one of the measures was picture quality. It didn't require a genius to note that, other than installation, the big issue would be picture quality. After six months of customer feedback, 80 per cent of the issues were picture quality. The area was so vast that none of our engineers could respond within any specific area. We launched a more comprehensive program that captured the various and specific facets of picture quality and service, and I can proudly say that the TELUS IP TV (Optik TV) offer today is second to none.

NIRVANA — SHAREHOLDER VALUE

The ultimate phase in CVM implementation is when the metrics are directly related to the actual share price and shareholder value. The harsh reality is that most organizations never get this far, and are stuck at phase one of data collection and the frustration of impotent executional ability.

SUMMARY

Beware of fake customer advocates, and CVM pretenders. Ensure that something as important as customer value and how you contribute to the bottom line are measures you can use and believe in. No matter where you are in the organization, if either for curiosity's sake or simply for the fact you care, get to know how your customers view you versus the competition. When you are genuinely working hard to contribute to the bottom line, make it your business to find out how you contribute and by how much.

Decisions in life are about compromise, be it value against purchase price or actions against your personal values and beliefs. My advice to you concerning work decisions is only compromise in things you care little about and not in things that are fundamental to you.

So if someone blows pretty smoke your way, know that it is still smoke and look for the substance from the smoke blower who is, needless to say, a first-class wanker.

If someone tells you a metric is important for business success or towards your performance, find out what it means to you or risk becoming an apprenticing wanker.

And if you care about how you contribute to the organization's success (and I hope you do) find out how you impact the business, or you are destined to go through your career as a wanker among wankers.

CHAPTER 11

Right, but not successful

Ibrahim Gedeon

ONE OF MY FAVOURITE questions is "do you want to be right or successful?" Some may say there is no difference. But as one gets older, one realizes there is a difference between being right and being successful. During the early part of one's career, being right usually meant being successful. As you become seasoned or go up the corporate ladder, some differences become evident based on the political climate in the corporation. When being successful is not the same as being right, the reason is frequently due to underlying politics and egos. Seldom is it due to business realities. Complex subjective aspects of corporate life come into play. By the way, being right makes you always feel good about yourself, so I have to admit there is also an element of personal satisfaction that comes into play.

Personally, there are certain things that I believe in, upon which I will not compromise. I have refused to learn the lesson of being politically correct at the expense of my beliefs and principles. For better or worse, it allows me to sleep well at night. I do have to qualify that the difference between one's ability to toe the corporate line versus adhering to personal beliefs can be influenced by the organization's political environment, and the level of honesty among colleagues or between managers and their teams.

I am proud to be counted, and I hope I am, among those who stood their ground, even at times when common sense suggested otherwise. By this I mean that there are times when the politically correct corporate line is the more politically "successful" one regardless of how wrong or not so right it is. I am not talking about disagreements on execution or priorities here. At the end of the day, we all work for someone and if they make the decision to pursue certain directions or interests, that is a privilege of leadership. The problem is that a lot of team members wind up doing a lot of things they disagree with. What I am referring to here is when things you hold dear in terms of principles and ethics have to be compromised, or when the truth is being misrepresented upwards to senior management ranks. I hate the expression the "emperor has no clothes" which indicates that the leader is clueless with what is happening around them. It also reflects negatively on the leadership team for not being honest with their boss.

An example where I stood my ground was when Nortel acquired Bay Networks. Nortel's Enterprise Data Networks division (EDN) was behind the acquisition. At that time, I was responsible for systems engineering and my role in the acquisition was to provide my assessment on the engineering capabilities. Bay Networks was much larger than Nortel's EDN and our counterparts at Bay were one or two levels higher in the hierarchy than ourselves (my counterpart was a vice president and I was a director – one lower in the corporate hierarchy).

My take was simple. I did not believe Bay Networks knew how to sell, support and care for telecommunication service providers, which by the way was the majority of the EDN clients and stakeholders. And I felt that the synergies were artificial and that our customers would see right through it. This was clearly not what the senior leadership team wanted to hear. They wanted a green light and enthusiasm that this was the best thing to happen. By the way, that acquisition with the right due diligence could have propelled Nortel into becoming a huge data IP equipment vendor giant.

I spent the next year in an organization that insisted the way things were done at Bay Networks was the better way, and they were the "sexy" IP company and Nortel was the boring legacy company. The focus was only on the competition – Cisco Networks – rather than the clients and marketplace. We lost R&D and sales momentum, as history attests, and I voiced my concern to all the Nortel executives I knew. At that time, Nortel was an organization that felt it could do nothing wrong. The stock was going through the roof, and the market capitalization was approaching $350 billion. Winston Estridge, EDN Executive Vice President of Sales at that time, called me "last man standing Gedeon." I am not sure if he was describing my act as one of stupidity, stubbornness, or admiration. Gut feel, it was one of the first two.

In the end, I like to think it was a case of good things coming to those who wait. We eventually ended up splitting the service provider and enterprise teams, which made sense to the people that mattered – our clients and employees. I have to say though that the time from acquiring Bay Networks to the time the enterprise and service provider teams were split was difficult for me. Adopting the corporate line that all was well in acquisition heaven would have been the path of lesser impedance. In the end, my team and I and our customers, enjoyed the benefits of re-structuring the teams. I was personally happier for having stood my ground. At the same time, I must confess that I often wonder if I would have been as outspoken if I had I emerged as the executive in charge of the combined organization!

I hasten to say that I am not sure that I can recommend this advice to everyone, as my next act of "stubbornness" resulted in me being let go (invited to leave is much nicer) from Nortel Networks. The official reason for my departure from Nortel was my chronic back pain, for which I actually ended up having two surgeries in 2003 and 2004. The real reason was my refusal to comply with corporate cosmetic changes. I forget whether it was the sixth or seventh round of layoffs. I had just had enough and wanted to manage my team according to business metrics rather than what appeared to look good. I received the "big dog" award for standing my ground and wanting to manage my team as a business, but it was less than a month later that I was told that I was not a team player. Leaving Nortel in 2003 was the best thing that happened to me, and I thank my president and CEO at that time for feeling that I was not a team player.

The point is simply that each one of us has some unique beliefs which define us. For me, when I cannot justify changes that the organization wants to implement, it is because I am sure that the changes are merely cosmetic, or because I am unable to understand and explain them to my team. Either way, one should leave in such situations, because at that juncture, jumping or being pushed is irrelevant; it is all good for both parties. I would like to point out, I am human and departing from over 11 years of friends, colleagues, and achievements at Nortel wasn't easy. But I believe that, given my loss of connectivity with the leadership team and its beliefs, remaining at Nortel would have alienated my team also, so I firmly believe it was all good.

SUMMARY

In a nutshell, we all have choices to make. I do not advocate absolute rigidity in life or in decision making, but when something seems wrong to you and contradicts your core beliefs, you are better off getting out of that organization. I do have to caution you that there is a fine line between being right and being the squeaky wheel in an organization, but if you truly believe something is wrong and no one is paying attention to it, make the effort to highlight and address what you think is wrong. Some additional advice, be explicit and provide solutions. There is nothing that I hate more than people whose comment is simply that they do not like something. To be credible, you have to also provide corrective plans. I have to point out, I am of these beliefs after 20 years of practice and experience so I would expect that those embarking on their careers take some time to firm up their core beliefs.

If, on the other hand, you feel you have made the effort and nothing results from your actions, you should leave the organization. History is clear here, you can rarely look the other way when things are wrong, hoping they self-correct. Things will come back to cause you grief, and there can be reams of reasons why things don't always work out, but at the end of the day, you need to be true to yourself when something just doesn't feel right.

So if you cannot sleep at night because you believe your leadership team is clueless, take action, and yes, leaving is an option. Otherwise, you're a wanker.

Similarly, if you see something you care for floundering, either try to change it, or leave, or else you are a wanker.

"I swear by my life, and my love of it, that I will never live for the sake of another man, nor ask another man to live for mine."
– AYN RAND, from *Atlas Shrugged*

Concluding Remarks

March 31st 2010, Cancun Mexico 14:06 local time.

LIFE HAS ALL KINDS of people and projects, and there are wankers everywhere. You and only you have to make the call to either go with the flow or do something about it. I hope that you find this condensed version of some of my career life experiences helpful no matter where you are in your own. If I leave you with a few thoughts, they are these: trusted and honest leadership is a must; empathy is a required skill; big projects must be well architected and hold clear business value, and make-work projects serve no one. Finally, invest in contributing to the organization in line with the corporate strategy and in a manner that involves resources at all levels. This is a privilege of leadership.

A final thought, I wrote this book to help others with a condensed version of my lessons hard learned and earned so they can apply some insight to their specific career challenges.

> *"Better to write for yourself and have no public than to write for the public and have no self."*
> – CYRIL CONNOLLY, editor emeritus of *Horizon Magazine*

Acknowledgements

THIS BOOK WOULD HAVE never happened without the encouragement of my friends and colleagues. I would like to single out a few people who made this journey with me: my uncle Jiryis Shammas, who provided invaluable and concise feedback and journeyed with me through six revisions; my previous TELUS boss and friend Barry Baptie, who poured through every detail of the book, providing direction and feedback (not always positive by the way), and my editor and friend Don Wells, who ensured the geek garbled messages are understood by most, if not all. And lastly, Kim Rasmussen, who without her coordination of the various pieces from written words into what you have today, this book would have never seen the light.

We are children of our environments and experiences, and I am not different. For that, I am eternally grateful to my TELUS team, colleagues, clients and leaders. You are the best.

Thanks, …ijg

To provide feedback check out www.ijgbooks.com

About the Author

ONE OF THE GLOBAL telecommunications industry's most colorful and respected executives, Ibrahim Gedeon has carved out an international career by combining equally large measures of skill in applied science, penetrating insight into a complex industry, and outright irreverence in sharing his thoughts and opinions. As Chief Technology Officer for TELUS, a leading national telecommunications company in Canada, his energy and engaging manner as a speaker and presenter are legendary within industry circles. Also renowned as a master chef and gregarious host, his Magnum Opus in the publishing world took the form of a cook book entitled From the Heart, released in 2005.

Ibrahim began his career in telecommunications engineering and research in 1990 when he joined Bell Northern Research, designing signal-processing software in the Cryptographic Systems division. He moved to Nortel Networks in 1994 as a network design engineer, where he provided technical network design expertise to a global customer base. He was named vice president and director of Data Network Engineering at Nortel in 1996; vice president of Internet Brand Management in 1999, and senior vice president of Wireless Engineering in 2000, where he led the global engineering team responsible for operations, sales support, and systems engineering. Sadly for both the author and his Nortel colleagues, he was also witness to the early stages of the tragic unraveling of Canada's global technology icon.

Ibrahim has held numerous leadership roles in the Institute of Electrical and Electronics Engineers (IEEE) and has also received numerous professional awards and various forms of industry recognition, including being named twice to the Global Telecoms Business magazine's "GTB Power 100," a list of the 100 most powerful and influential people in the telecoms industry.

He joined Vancouver, BC based TELUS in 2003. In his role as CTO he is responsible for technology strategy, service and network architecture, service delivery and operational support systems for the company's wire line and wireless divisions, as well as service and network convergence, enterprise applications and network infrastructure strategies and evolution.

Ibrahim is currently the General Chair for the 2012 IEEE International Conference on Communications in Ottawa and also serves on the board of a number of industry associations, including the Washington, DC based Alliance for Telecommunications Industry.

A native of Lebanon, he has a bachelor's in electrical engineering from the American University of Beirut and a Masters' in Electronics Engineering from Carleton University. He received a Honourary Doctor of Laws degree in 2010 from the University of British Columbia. He currently resides in Edmonton, Alberta.